WISDOM FROM THE WEALTHY DEAD

Wisdom From the Wealthy Dead

A Medium Interviews the Souls of Three American Tycoons

SHIRLEY SMOLKO, MBA, MSA

Cavallaro Publishing

COPYRIGHT NOTICE

Wisdom From the Wealthy Dead: A Medium Interviews the Souls of Three American Tycoons

Copyright ©2022 Shirley Smolko. All rights reserved.

No part of this publication may be reproduced, distributed, or transmitted in any form or by any means, including photocopying, recording, or other electronic or mechanical methods, without the prior written permission of the publisher or author, except in the case of brief quotations embodied in reviews and certain other noncommercial uses permitted by copyright law.

Cover Design by Shirley Smolko

Printed in the U.S.A.

First Printing 2022

ISBN: 978-1-7345146-5-0

Library of Congress Control Number: 2022919437

Cavallaro Publishing

North Venice, FL.

www.cavallaropub.com

cavallaropub@gmail.com

CONTENTS

COPYRIGHT NOTICE - v
ACKNOWLEDGEMENT - ix
DISCLAIMER - xi
WHO THIS BOOK IS FOR - xiii
PREFACE - xv

~ 1 ~
Wisdom of the Wealthy
1

~ 2 ~
Hetty Green's Interview
13

~ 3 ~
Hetty Tells Her Story
25

~ 4 ~
Shedding Light on the Miserly Hetty
32

~ 5 ~
The Wealth Consciousness of Hetty Green
43

~ 6 ~

The Commodore's Interview

54

~ 7 ~

The Commodore Tells His Story

64

~ 8 ~

Shedding Light on the Mystical Commodore

73

~ 9 ~

The Wealth Consciousness of The Commodore

76

~ 10 ~

J. D. Rockefeller's Interview

88

~ 11 ~

John Tells His Story

96

~ 12 ~

Shedding Light on the Religious Rockefeller

104

~ 13 ~

The Wealth Consciousness of John D. Rockefeller

109

EPILOGUE - 127

ABOUT THE AUTHOR - 131

ACKNOWLEDGEMENT

I would like to acknowledge my wonderful, loving, and supportive husband, Joe, who worked diligently to edit this book. He has always encouraged me in my writing endeavors and work as a psychic medium. There was a time early in our relationship, before we were married, when he told me he believed that when you're dead, you're dead. He's changed his mind!

DISCLAIMER

The publisher and author make no guarantees or promises that the information contained in this book will give you all the wisdom you need to be a wise entrepreneur or investor. Nor do they make any promises or guarantees that you will become wealthy by using the ideas in this book.

Additionally, they make no guarantees as to the accuracy, quality, or completeness of the information contained herein and will not be responsible or liable for any errors, omissions, or reader's reliance on the information. The opinions of the souls in this book are expressly their own as the author is just the conduit for their comments, and not the source.

WHO THIS BOOK IS FOR

This book is for entrepreneurs, investors, business students, and anyone looking for the same financial and business wisdom that tycoons, throughout the ages, have used to amass great wealth. This wisdom is as applicable today as it was during the ancient times of King Solomon and the era of the second industrial revolution—known as the Gilded Age.

The three tycoons in this book were not the first to have used the wisdom contained within these pages. Ancient tycoons such as Augustus Caesar, King Solomon, Alan Rufus, Genesis Khan, and Emperor Shenzong of Song all amassed great wealth using the same wisdom.

Hetty Green acquired a great deal of wealth wisdom from her father and Grandfather Gideon. Unlike Vanderbilt and Rockefeller, she inherited a significant amount of money from her father—$1,000,000 in cash with the remainder of his estate in trust, which she was not allowed to manage. She took this $1,000,000 and turned it into $100,000,000 before her death in 1916. Cornelius Vanderbilt and John D. Rockefeller inherited very little—if any—money, and most of the wealth wisdom they acquired seemed to have come from common sense and intuition. The one thing all three had in common was their consciousness of wealth as evidenced by their personality traits, thoughts, and behaviors regarding money and success.

It doesn't matter whether you believe in mediums or not, the wisdom contained within the pages of this book is timeless and may help you become a captain of industry in your own right.

PREFACE

Channeling The Wisdom Of The Wealthy Dead

As a psychic medium, I can communicate with spirits in the afterworld and relay their messages to people in the physical world. Recently, the practice of mediumship has been gaining popularity through shows like "The Long Island Medium," "Monica the Medium," "Mama Medium," and "The Hollywood Medium." People are often skeptical of mediums until they have a reading that provides them with valid evidence that can't be disputed.

There are two types of mediumship: mental and physical. Mental mediumship, also known as psychic mediumship, uses the medium's consciousness to communicate information through extrasensory perceptions such as clairvoyance (seeing), clairaudience (hearing), clairsentience (touch), clairempathy (emotions), clairolfactory (smell), and clairgustance (taste). Physical mediumship is more or less associated with the religious practice of Spiritualism. Raps, ectoplasm, levitation, and materialization are said to occur when the spiritualist medium is communicating with spirits. Spiritualist mediums are individuals who participate in the spiritualist religion and may or may not have any genuine mediumistic ability. Psychic mediums, including myself, are not usually associated with a Spiritualist Church, nor do we practice their methods or hold the same beliefs.

Like most legitimate psychic mediums, I was born open to the spirit world. I have been able to perceive spirits and psychic information for as long as I can remember. I came by my abilities honestly. Both my mother and father had abilities. My mother was what I call a sleeping medium. Spirits visited and gave her messages through her dreams. My father could see and communicate with spirits while wide awake. His abilities occurred spontaneously so often throughout the day that I began to wonder if he might be schizophrenic. While I was studying psychiatric nursing, I researched the DSM (*Diagnostic and Statistical Manual of Mental Disorders*) to determine if he suffered from any form of mental illness. Fortunately, his behaviors didn't fit any of the categories for schizophrenia or any other mental illness, mainly because he was always completely grounded and could distinguish physical reality from spiritual reality.

My parents divorced when I was a toddler, and my mother, brother, and I went to live with my Grandma Nora. Being very religious, she tolerated but did not encourage my abilities. Early in life, I learned that I had to hide my gift from people outside the family. At the age of twelve, I made the mistake of giving a message from spirit to my grandmother in front of one of her zealous religious friends—Rose. My grandmother's brother, Joe, who had just passed away, appeared to me with a message to give Nora. I was so excited about his appearance that I immediately ran to my grandmother and delivered the message. Upon delivering the message, Rose aggressively reprimanded me by saying, "You stop that; that comes from the devil, and you are a witch! That's Satanism!" My reply to her was, "I am neither a witch nor a Satanist. I love God, and I go to Sunday school every week." After this incident, I continued to give messages, both psychic and mediumistic, to members of my family, but I made sure I hid my abilities from the outside world. It would be many years after the deaths of my grandparents and parents that I would entertain the thought of using my abilities to help people outside my family. Television shows like *The Long Island Medium* and *The Hollywood Medium*—which helped to increase the acceptance of psychic mediums—made me feel more comfortable about embracing my abilities for public service.

Some psychic mediums also use writing to channel information from spirits. This technique is known as automatic writing and is often used in conjunction with the Clairs mentioned above. Psychic mediums Theresa Caputo (the Long Island Medium), Tyler Henry (the Hollywood Medium), and Monica Ten-Kate (Monica the Medium) use some automatic writing on their TV shows to help them deliver messages. Although I can channel information through automatic writing, I prefer to stick with the Clairs for individual and gallery event readings, but to write this book, I have combined both techniques.

I don't have to offer services as a psychic medium to make a living. I can do that in any number of ways, including nursing. I give readings because I love giving readings. It brings me much joy to provide healing to the bereaved by connecting them with their deceased loved ones.

Most spirits come to me to relay their messages to the living; however, some come to me just to tell their story. Most of my retro-cognitive dreams have occurred as a result of spirits wanting to tell me their story (I have written about some of these stories in previous books). I have been able to validate many of these stories through historical records such as the census, newspaper articles, and books. I believe these spirits were looking for absolution through confession, while others just wanted to set the record straight about their lives (these spirits knew that I would be publishing their stories to the world long before I did). As any good medium or psychotherapist would do, I allowed them to vent their concerns and tell me their stories.

When English-speaking spirits talk to me, I hear them in their voice, dialect, and all. For instance, Cornelius communicates with me using English which sounds similar to some of the "choppy" dialects used in *The Adventures of Huckleberry Finn*. Of course, he also uses quite a bit of profanity. Like Cornelius, Hetty uses a lot of contractions, *such as ain't* and *can't*, along with an occasional *thee* or *thou*, as well as some profanity. John has a dialect similar to the other two but speaks more slowly and deliberately. He tends to be soft-spoken and never uses profanity. Their use of the English language was common in America during the nineteenth century but may be more difficult to understand in the twenty-first century. To promote clarity and make it easier for me to write, I have transcribed their messages using modern English. In the cases of Cornelius and Hetty, I have cut out most of their profanity—especially Cornelius.

Ever since I can remember, I have had a love affair with books. Not only do I enjoy reading them, but I also love writing them. Writing this book has allowed me to combine my love of writing with my passion for channeling spirits by telling their stories. I can't think of any better way to spend my day than writing a book channeled by Spirit (unless I'm playing golf with my husband).

Because someone forgot to issue my privilege card when I was born, I grew up in a very poor family. I understand firsthand how poverty thinking can beget more poverty. The only way to overcome poverty is to change negative thoughts and beliefs about wealth and money. It took me many years to overcome the stinking poverty thinking that I acquired from my family of origin. As I learned more about wealth consciousness and the truth that I can be both spiritual and rich, I was able to shift my beliefs and mindset, which, combined with faith, increased prosperity in my life. I hope this book will give you the insights and inspiration you need to create your own empire of wealth.

~ 1 ~

WISDOM OF THE WEALTHY

"Wisdom is the principal thing; therefore get wisdom: and with all thy getting get understanding."

—Proverbs 4:7 (KJV)

Wisdom is obtained when factual knowledge is acquired and the rationale behind the facts is thoroughly understood. Wisdom often comes with experience but can be learned. You don't have to make your own mistakes. Instead, you can avoid them by learning from the experiences of others. The wisdom of the wealthy is there for the taking. Choose to take it and open yourself up to a whole new way of thinking, which will allow you to achieve the financial success you deserve.

Thoughts are a vital force. Although they are unseen, they are actual things, as real as the wind. They can come from within or without, and their value to any mind depends on the conditioning of that mind. You make your own poverty or wealth by the thoughts you think, which are the result of your past thoughts as well as the thoughts passed down to you from your ancestors. Your current thoughts will mold your future condition, so choose them wisely.

Poverty Consciousness

According to the Collins Online Dictionary, *wisdom* is the ability to use experience and knowledge to make sensible decisions or judgments. According to the following statistics, it is obvious that most Americans lack the experience and knowledge (wisdom) that create wealth. At the time of this writing, in America, it is estimated that:

- 78% of U.S. workers live paycheck to paycheck to make ends meet.
- 28% of Americans have no emergency fund at all.
- 25% do not have enough to cover three months of expenses.
- Only 32% keep a household budget.
- Only 16% of young people said they were optimistic about their financial future.
- 54% of young people said they were worried that they wouldn't be able to pay back their student loans.

These are sad and discouraging statistics. I think the primary reason most Americans live paycheck to paycheck is that they have a poverty consciousness. Having a poverty consciousness means accepting and believing in thoughts that create poverty. Most poor people believe nothing will ever change for them or their children; therefore, they should make peace with their lot in life. Individuals with this mindset believe wealth and social mobility are not within their grasp, so they create and perpetuate behaviors that reinforce their consciousness of poverty. The following list contains the most common thoughts and behaviors (known as personality traits) associated with poverty consciousness:

Thought #1: All rich people are going to hell.

Behavior: Avoids financial and wealth education.

Thought #2: Rich people are crooked and can't be trusted.

Behavior: Suspicious regarding the motives of rich people, which causes further polarization from a consciousness of wealth.

Thought #3: I have to have a job to earn money.

Behavior: Works for an employer instead of self.

Thought #4: I can't save money because it takes all my money to live.

Behavior: Does not look for ways to save money; saving money is not a priority.

Thought #5: I can't make over a certain amount of money or I'll lose my government benefit.

Behavior: Looks for ways to avoid making more money.

Thought #6: I have to get a good education so that I can get a good job.

Behavior: Works for money instead of having money work for them.

Thought #7: Only rich people make investments.

Behavior: Doesn't look for ways to invest money.

Thought #8: I have to make sure I keep my money safe.

Behavior: Refuses to invest money or take calculated risks to make their money work for them.

Thought #9: The only way I can get rich is through good luck.

Behavior: Buys lottery tickets instead of learning strategies for becoming rich.

Thought #10: I can't afford the best foods.

Behavior: Eats a lot of fast and junk food instead of fruits and vegetables.

Thought #11: I don't have time to exercise because I work all the time and then I'm too tired.

Behavior: Does not pursue a healthy lifestyle, which may eventually lead to illness and more financial distress.

Habits evolve from persistent thoughts, which manifest into behaviors that are nearly or completely involuntary. Habitual thoughts are usually passed from generation to generation, which makes it very difficult to break the thought patterns that create poverty. The perception that rich people are inherently evil and are going to hell because they have a lot of money makes it even more difficult to break through the poverty mindset. The truth is, the wealthy aren't inherently evil just because they have money. Yes, there are evil rich people, but there are also evil poor people. Putting evil people and rich people in the same category simply because rich people have money is irrational.

Wealth Consciousness

The real difference between the wealthy and poor is not their lifestyle but their beliefs and thoughts about wealth, as evidenced by their behaviors. Thus, rich people have behaviors that are based on a way of thinking about wealth that is completely different from that of poor people. The beginning of wealth consciousness starts by identifying and assimilating the same thoughts and behaviors that have brought countless others wealth throughout the ages. The following list contains the most common thoughts and behaviors that I perceive are associated with wealth consciousness:

Thought #1: Poverty is the root of all evil.

Behavior: Engages in activities to learn how to acquire wealth.

Thought #2: I have the right to be rich.

Behavior: Pursues wealth with great determination.

Thought #3: Rich people are ambitious.

Behavior: Sets goals.

Thought #4: Entrepreneurship is the fastest way to create wealth.

Behavior: Builds one or more businesses.

Thought #5: Money is a resource that must not be wasted.

Behavior: Keeps an accurate record of every penny coming in and going out; may exhibit frugality.

Thought #6: I must have cash on hand so I can take advantage of opportunities when they come knocking.

Behavior: May park cash in money market accounts for quick liquidity, but with higher interest than regular savings accounts, or may arrange for a line of credit.

Thought #7: I must put my money to work to make more money.

Behavior: Looks for investments that will yield the most profit with the least risk.

Thought #8: I need to pass my wealth to my loved ones so they will be taken care of and continue to manage the money I leave them.

Behavior: Creates a will and trust for loved ones.

Thought #9: For my loved ones to manage the money I leave them, they will need to have a financial education.

Behavior: Passes knowledge of wealth creation to children or arranges for them to have a formal financial education.

Thought #10: I have to take care of my health, so I'll be around to take care of my family and finances.

Behavior: Establishes and maintains good health habits by eating nutritious foods, getting plenty of sleep, and exercising.

Building wealth is like building a house. Before you can build a house, you must draw up a blueprint that contains every room in it. Every created object takes form in the same way. The creative principle of the universe is the mind, and thought is the building material it uses. Behaviors are the tools that result from thoughts, which work to build the house.

Impact of Religion on Wealth Consciousness

Religious people often misquote scriptures such as I Timothy 6:10, which states, "The love of money is the root of all evil." The love of money itself is not evil, nor is the acquisition of it. The willingness to commit a crime to get money is the root of evil.

Another scripture that some religious people often misunderstand is Matthew 19:24 (KJV): "And again I say unto you, It is easier for a camel to go through the eye of a needle than for a rich man to enter the kingdom of God." I believe what Christ was saying in this passage is that it is hard for a rich man to enter into the kingdom (the spiritual kingdom of manifestation) if he puts his faith in his riches and not in the Spirit.

In the parable of the Talents (Matthew 25:14-30 NKJV), Christ gave the mandate that we must create wealth. Jesus delivered this parable to his disciples before entering Jerusalem, where he knew he would be crucified:

> 14 For the kingdom of heaven is like a man traveling to a faraway country who called his servants and delivered his goods to them.
>
> 15 And to one he gave five talents, to another two, and to another one, each according to his own ability, and immediately he went on a journey.
>
> 16 Then he who had received the five talents went and traded with them and made another five talents.
>
> 17 And likewise, he who had received two gained two more also.
>
> 18 But he who had received one went and dug in the ground and hid his lord's money.
>
> 19 After a long time, the lord of those servants came and settled accounts with them.
>
> 20 So he who had received five talents came and brought five other talents, saying, "Lord, you delivered to me five talents; look, I have gained five more talents besides them."

21 His lord said to him, "Well done, good and faithful servant; you were faithful over a few things; I will make you ruler over many things. Enter into the joy of your Lord."

22 He who had received two talents came and said, "Lord, you delivered to me two talents; look, I have gained two more talents besides them."

23 His lord said to him, "Well done, good and faithful servant; you have been faithful over a few things; I will make you ruler over many things. Enter into the joy of your Lord."

24 Then he who had received the one talent came and said, "Lord, I knew you to be a hard man, reaping where you have not sown and gathering where you have not scattered seed.

25 And I was afraid, so I went and hid your talent in the ground. Look, there you have what is yours."

26 But his lord answered and said to him, "You wicked and lazy servant, you knew that I reap where I have not sown and gather where I have not scattered seed.

27 So you ought to have deposited my money with the bankers, and at my coming, I would have received back my own with interest.

28 So take the talent from him and give it to him, who has ten talents.

29 For to everyone who has, more will be given, and he will have abundance; but from him who does not have, even what he has will be taken away.

30 And cast the unprofitable servant into the outer darkness. There will be weeping and gnashing of teeth."

I know firsthand that this parable has been misinterpreted by many ministers, who preach that it refers to abilities rather than money. This parable also occurs again in Luke 19:12-17 and uses the word *minas* instead of talents. According to the online Oxford English Dictionary, a *talent* is the value of a talent weight (of gold, silver, etc.): money of account. So, this parable refers to money, not abilities, which makes a lot more sense than making it about an ability. Viewing a talent as money also makes it congruent with the Luke version of the parable.

While riches have been condemned by many Western religions as dangerous to man's spiritual growth, most churches have always welcomed the affluent to help them support their ministry. How can money be evil when no one, not even religious people, can do without it? If money makes us evil, why does God give us wealth, as suggested in the following scriptures?

> But thou shalt remember the Lord thy God; for it is He that giveth thee power to get wealth, that He may establish His covenant, which He swore unto thy fathers, as it is this day. (Deuteronomy 8:18 KJV)
>
> I will certainly give you the wisdom and knowledge you requested. But I will also give you wealth, riches, and fame such as no other king has had before you or will ever have in the future!" (2 Chronicles 1:12, New Living Translation)

Prosperity gospel preaching grew out of the New Thought movement of the late nineteenth and early twentieth centuries. New Thought teaches that the power of God resides within us and that we can use it to create the life we want. Just as God created the world using thought, people can shape their world with their thoughts. Positive thoughts yield positive circumstances, and negative thoughts yield negative situations. Practitioners of New Thought believe in the divinity of the individual soul and the power of the mind over matter. In other words, you have the power of the Creator within you; therefore, you can intentionally make changes in your physical reality by channeling this Power through thought with faith.

In the years following World War II, some evangelists began to preach about miraculous healings and supernatural financial blessings. Successes were heralded as evidence of the truth of their version of the gospel. Failures could be blamed on a lack of faith among those seeking miracles. This type of preaching became known as prosperity theology, which viewed the Bible as a contract between God and his children and taught that if we have faith in God, he will deliver health and prosperity. This doctrine emphasizes the importance of personal empowerment and teaches that it is God's will for his people to be blessed. Sickness and poverty are viewed as curses to be broken by faith.

Wise Captains of Industry or Robber Barrons?

My intent in writing this book is not to pass judgment on these tycoons as to whether or not they were robber barons or captains of industry. This ongoing debate will continue long after I am gone. There are pros and cons to every decision we make or action we take in life, and business is no different. My goal in interviewing the wealthy dead is to reveal their thoughts about wealth, the actions they took to achieve it, and the things they would do differently if given a chance to create wealth again. My objective is to identify the common behaviors associated with the mindset of each of these wealthy tycoons. The mindset of the rich is often referred to as *wealth consciousness.* The theory of *wealth consciousness* holds that if an individual's philosophy about money is one of abundance, then it will be drawn to them through their thoughts and actions.

During the Gilded Age of the post-Civil War era (1870-1900), except for two recessions—one in the mid-1870s and the other during the mid-1890s—the U.S. economy grew at a phenomenal rate.

Every aspect of the American economy expanded, from traditional activities to new enterprises brought about by the huge influx of cutting-edge technological inventions. The gross national product practically doubled, and the per capita GNP increased by 35 percent. Wages increased by 20 percent, and a new middle class emerged for the first time in the history of the United States. Manufacturing output increased by 180 percent, steel production grew to over 10,000,000 tons per year by 1900, and railroad miles increased by 113 percent. The overall increase in train service may have acted as a catalyst for increasing output because manufacturers were able to supply more of their products to meet consumer demand.

Large cities emerged as people moved from rural to urban areas and immigrants arrived from around the world to work in the ever-expanding factories. For example, the population of Chicago multiplied from 30,000 people in 1850 to over 1,700,000 by 1900. During the same period, the population of New York City increased from just over 500,000 to over 3,000,000. In 1871, Birmingham, Alabama, evolved into a city built upon the thriving steel industry. Skyscrapers also emerged, changing the landscape of many cities.

Although many enterprising and visionary businesspeople have been credited with bringing about the economic prosperity of the Gilded Age, I have chosen—what I believe to be—three of the most notable ones to be included in this book: John D. Rockefeller, oil magnate; Cornelius Vanderbilt, transportation magnate; and Hetty Green, financier to the government, churches, and businessmen. These three top the list of a group of industrialists often identified as the "captains of industry" (business leaders whose means of amassing a personal fortune contributed positively to the country in some way). They were individuals with vision, time, and money whose activities helped to grow our nation.

The term "robber baron" was applied to powerful nineteenth-century industrialists who were viewed as having used questionable practices to amass their wealth. Some feel that the powerful industrialists of the gilded age should be referred to as robber barons. This view portrays the above-mentioned tycoons as ruthless businesspeople who would stop at nothing to achieve great wealth. They were accused of unfair practices such as influencing high levels of government, paying subsistence wages, providing poor working conditions, squashing competition by creating monopolies, and creating schemes to sell stocks at inflated prices to unsuspecting investors.

Careful economic research on most "robber barons" shows that they were neither robbers nor barons. They didn't rob; they acquired their money the old-fashioned way—they started businesses. Many of these so-called robber barons, like Vanderbilt, Rockefeller, and Green, started their businesses from scratch and were not granted any special privileges. So, why were the tycoons of the Gilded Age accused of being robber barons? Were they all bad? Didn't they help grow a nation, increase the Gross National Product, and create jobs that may not have otherwise been provided? In my opinion, the popular press had much to do with demonizing and promoting a distorted view of these tycoons. For example, Ida Tarbell, the famous "muckraker," gave Rockefeller lousy press because she had witnessed her father (Frank Tarbell, an oil producer and refiner) lose out in competition to Rockefeller. As a result, the luxurious lifestyle she and her family were experiencing came to an end. I believe Tarbell held a grudge and was able to get revenge through the negative press. Hetty Green was demonized by the media because she was an assertive and successful businesswoman in a time when men ruled the business world. Of the three, it is my opinion that Vanderbilt wasn't demonized to the degree that Rockefeller and Green were, but he was sensationalized as being a vulgar and mean-spirited man. The press hasn't changed a lot since the gilded age. To this day, the rich are still sensationalized by the media.

~ 2 ~

HETTY GREEN'S INTERVIEW

"A good businesswoman is often sharper than a good businessman"
—Hetty Green

Witch of Wall Street
Library of Congress

Hetty's Interview: Part I

This is the section Hetty has been waiting for. She has been very patient but is now extremely eager to start the interview. During breakfast this morning, she kept whispering in my ear for me to hurry because it was time to start. So, without further ado, we begin the long-awaited interview with Hetty Green.

    Thank you for agreeing to do this interview with me, Mrs. Green.

    "Please just call me Hetty. Labels and formalities are not necessary, and I was raised not to use them."

    Okay, I'll call you Hetty.

Q: Did you ever feel rejected or unloved by your parents?

A: When they sent me to my Grandpa Gideon's house, I felt that they didn't love me because I was a girl and they wanted a boy. It bothered me for a long time, but, eventually, I proved to them that I was smarter than most boys and had a better head for business than most men.

Q: Do you have any resentment towards your parents for sending you to live with your Grandfather Gideon?

A: No, not anymore. My mother was ill with hysteria, and my father could not care for me, so I understand why they would send me to my grandfather's house to be cared for. My Aunt Sylvia did her best to look after my best interests while I was there, but she was sick too and limited in the care that she could give me. I had a nanny who looked after most of my needs.

Q: Did you ever accompany your father on his business rounds?

A: When I was a little older, my father took on the rounds of his whaling fleet and showed me how to keep the accounts of expenses and income.

Q: What did your father teach you about making a business profitable?

A: He taught me the importance of frugality and controlling expenses.

Q: I understand you read the financial section of the newspaper to your Grandfather Gideon every evening. Did he teach you how to interpret the reports?

A: Yes, he also taught me what makes a good investment and how to stay away from bad ones.

Q: Did your father open a bank account for you when you were a child?

A: I opened my own savings account with the money I saved from my allowance.

Q: How often did you contribute to your bank account?

A: I made a deposit every month when I was home and periodic deposits when I was away at school. Nonetheless, I saved my money and deposited it as often as I could get to the bank.

Q: Growing up, were you made to wear plain clothing?

A: All Quakers wore plain clothing. It was frowned upon for men or women to spend money on unnecessary frills such as clothes with ruffles, lace, or ribbons.

Q: I understand you were almost 33 years old before you married. Many women of your generation married at a much younger age. Why did you marry so late?

A: I didn't meet anybody of worth who caught my fancy before Edward Henry came along. I did enjoy living a single life and doing as I pleased. I had no problem staying single; but my father, on the other hand, held certain expectations of me, which I had to honor. Plus, I wasn't getting any younger.

Q: In the lawsuit over your Aunt Sylvia's will, the expert witness at the trial testified that the copy of the will you produced was a forgery. Soon after the trial you and your husband sailed to London where you lived for seven years. Did you move to London, because you feared getting arrested for forgery?

A: Yes, I thought there was a great possibility I might get arrested. I didn't want to give them the opportunity or pleasure of doing that. You know, I am a very proactive person, so I decided to make the move as quickly as possible. My husband was in total agreement with me.

Q: As a child raised in the Quaker religion, were you taught against the use of lawsuits?

A: I believed in an eye for an eye. I was raised to settle things away from the courts of law, but I quickly learned that didn't always work, especially if you are a woman.

Q: Did you ever have servants?

A: I had as many as I needed, and that was enough. It was hard to find reliable help you could trust. Later in life, I ended up having a secretary who assisted me, along with a housekeeper.

Q: Why did you leave your husband but remain married?

A: I loved Edward Henry, but I couldn't allow him to steal from me. He crossed a line when he had the banker withdraw money from my account without even asking! I had already bailed him out on several occasions, and he knew I was done, but he took my money anyway. I couldn't live with someone I can't trust! I stayed married to him because he was my children's father, and I did not want to publicly dishonor him, so I put him up at the Union Club in New York. He lived in style but on a budget.

Q: I heard that in addition to being a spendthrift, your husband was also a philanderer who spent lots of money on other women. Was it true?

A: My husband was a spendthrift, and as far as being a philanderer, he was just generous, not only to women but to everyone.

Q: It was reported in several newspapers that, as a grown man, Ned had to have his leg amputated because of an injury that occurred while sledding when he was a boy. They say it's your fault because you didn't want to spend money on his treatment. Is it true that you didn't seek treatment for Ned because you wanted to avoid the medical expense?

A: No, it's not true! I never withheld any good thing from my children, especially medical care. My children were the most precious gift I ever received, and I treasured them above all. I was afraid the doctors would try to take Ned's leg as a boy, and I just couldn't allow them to do that to him. He was very physically active growing up. He played all kinds of sports with his friends and was a happy child. I trusted God and nature to mend Ned's knee without the aid of the surgeon's blade.

Q: It was also reported that you wouldn't heat your bedroom because you didn't want to pay the fuel expense. Is this true?

A: No, it's not true; I had plenty of coal to burn. I didn't get up throughout the night to add fuel to the fireplace, and neither did my housekeeper. Sleeping in a cool room was beneficial to my health, and besides, I stayed very warm under many layers of quilts.

Q: Later in life, you were baptized into the Episcopalian faith. Why did you become an Episcopalian?

A: My husband had been raised as an Episcopalian and was buried in an Episcopalian cemetery. I wanted to be buried with him, so I had to convert to his religion to do so.

Q: Did you raise your children in the Quaker tradition?

A: I raised them with many of the same values I was raised with, but I did not require them to practice as Quakers or attend the Friends Meeting House.

Q: Being such a successful businesswoman, you must have endured a lot of pain and abuse from men, especially envious men. How did you deal with them?

A: I looked them straight in the eye and let them know that I was a force to be reckoned with. When I was done giving them a piece of my mind, they knew they couldn't mess with Hetty Green and get away with it! I knew how to take up for myself in business and in court!

Q: There were rumors that you obtained a permit to carry a handgun. Is this true?

A: Yes, I carried a handgun in my purse. I had to protect myself. The streets of New York City were filled with vagabonds, thieves, and thugs of all kinds. I understand that not much has changed since I've been on this side of life.

Q: Were you a good shot?

A: I was very accurate. When I was just a girl, my Grandfather Gideon showed me how to sight in, use, and care for a muzzleloader.

Q: How did you feel about women not having the right to vote?

A: I felt that it was wrong. I was mistreated by men all my life and wanted to see women have the right to vote. If given a chance, women can demonstrate superior insight and judgment; however, most of the common women of my day showed no interest in anything other than the drudgeries of their daily existence. Many of them were preoccupied with the struggle to feed and clothe a multitude of children, and they didn't care about whether or not they had the right to vote.

Q: Did you participate in the suffragette movement?

A: No, I had business to take care of that occupied all of my time. Of course, I didn't like the way men treated women during my physical life, but what could I do? I'm not responsible for other women. They need to stand up for themselves. All women should do what I did—show the men folk that a woman can be better at taking care of business than they are. That's what I did! Huh, I had incompetent men begging me for loans. Most of these men—including my husband—were complete and utter failures at business. They thought I might be naive enough to give them my money so they could lose it too with no way to pay me back, no capital, no nothing! They quickly discovered that I was no fool!

Q: You took the cash inheritance from your father, which was initially about $919,000 in liquid assets, and turned it into an estate estimated at $100,000,000. I'm sure the base amount you started with was much less than the amount you inherited, especially after having to use your money to bail your husband out of bad business speculations, not to mention the large amount of money he embezzled from your account—with the help of his bankers—so he could cover even more losses without your knowledge. Nevertheless, you still managed to amass a fortune. How did you do it?

A: I had a thorough understanding of business and investing. I also used a lot of common sense and listened to my gut to help me along the way.

Q: What did you invest in?

A: I mainly invested in real estate, bonds, mines, and railroads.

Q: How did you make money from your investments?

A: I made money by buying real estate at a low price and selling it at a high price. I bought municipal bonds which paid dividends, gold mines that brought a nice profit, and mortgages always backed by property that yielded high returns. With Ned's help and oversight, I also bought distressed, mismanaged railroads at rock-bottom prices and turned them into very profitable lines.

Q: What was your stock trading strategy?

A: I didn't speculate in stock. Speculating in the stock market is a fool's game operated by men who waste no time in manipulating the misinformed right out of their money; however, I did buy railroad stocks that I thought had the potential for great growth.

Q: I understand that you were a financier. What types of loans did you make?

A: I only loaned money that was backed by capital, such as real estate or a business.

Q: To whom did you loan money?

A: I made loans to private businesses, churches, and the government.

Q: Did the interest you charge vary according to the type of borrower?

A: Yes, it did.

Q: Why did you charge different interest rates?

A: The government is the safest of all three to lend to because they never default on their loans, so they got the lowest rate. Churches are next in line because of their morals and work for the Lord, they are unlikely to default, so they get the next-lowest rate. Businesses get the absolute highest rate because they are most likely to default.

Q: I understand you accepted mortgages on some of the loans you made. Did you ever foreclose on any of these mortgages?

A: Unfortunately I had to. Business is business, and I wouldn't have been a successful businesswoman if I didn't take proper action.

Q: In addition to New York, I understand you had a lot of real estate in places like Chicago, Massachusetts, Vermont, Texas, and San Francisco. Why did you buy so much property in other states?

A: Because everything was expanding west, and I knew I could buy cheaply ahead of demand and sell dearly upon demand. Even in cities that were settled and greatly populated, such as New York and Chicago, property values continued to rise, and there were always many profit opportunities.

Q: How many hours each day did you devote to the business?

A: I worked from sun up to sun down every day of the week except Sundays. I used Sundays to get caught up with my reading on current and emerging business industries. I also took time to spend with my family and reflect on business affairs.

Q: Did you ever feel you had something to prove by amassing a great fortune?

A: I was told early in childhood that I would have to be responsible for taking care of my business affairs when I grew up. Most all Quaker women are engaged in some type of business enterprise and are expected to be successful at it, whether it's selling preserves, quilts, or some other product at the town market or organizing some activist activity.

I knew that my father was very disappointed that I was born a girl instead of a boy. The next child born was a son, but he died within a few weeks of birth. My father became an angry person after this, and my mother retreated into a world of sadness and detachment from life, so there were no further attempts to have children. I was sent to my Grandfather Gideon's house to be cared for. My grandfather taught me everything he knew about business and investing. He made me feel special like, I could accomplish anything as good as or better than a boy. So, to answer your question, I didn't feel as if I had anything to prove by amassing a great fortune. It was my responsibility to take care of my business affairs, and it was a sign of God's blessing that I amassed a great fortune.

Q: What qualities do you believe an individual must have to be successful in amassing wealth?

A: For individuals to be successful in amassing wealth, they must have a sound knowledge of business operations. They must also have a thorough knowledge of how investment channels work and know when to buy and sell to secure a profit. You always make money when you buy, so buy cheap and sell higher. You don't have to be greedy to make a profit. It is important to get your profit and get out before the price hits its high point and starts crashing down, especially with real estate. Don't get caught buying into the bubble. This is when you should be selling! Buy your investments when no one wants them, then wait until everybody wants them and sell them dearly.

Q: This sounds like *contrarian investing,* also known as *value investing.* One of the twentieth century's greatest investors, Warren Buffett, used this technique to amass his fortune. I think he emulated your style. Do you have a name for the way you invested?

A: I don't think there was a name for the way I invested, but *contrarian investing* sounds good to me! I was always somewhat of a contrarian by nature. I bought things cheaply when nobody else wanted them and then sold them when everybody was crazy to have them. I used a lot of common sense and listened to what my gut was telling me.

Q: If you could do it all over again, would you do anything differently?

A: I did everything that I was supposed to do. There's nothing I would do differently.

Q: Do you have any regrets about your life?

A: I have no regrets. I did the best I could as Hetty Green. I experienced physical life and learned the lessons I was supposed to learn.

Q: Do you have any plans for reincarnation?

A: I have no plans for reincarnation. Why would I? My life is so lovely here, and there is no strife of any kind. Everything I could ever want or need is here in this wonderful Summerland of Heaven!

Q: What financial advice would you give to female investors of the twenty-first century?

A: Know that you can do anything as well or better than any man. As a woman, you have inherent qualities such as the tendency to nurture and protect all that you give birth to, whether it be children or businesses. Men, on the other hand, who generally lack the nurturing proclivities of women, tend to operate a business like a bull in a china shop.

Thank you, Hetty. That concludes the first part of our interview. In the second part, I would like you to tell your life story from your perspective. We'll do that in a day or so after we have had sufficient time to rest and recharge our batteries.

~ 3 ~

HETTY TELLS HER STORY

"There is no great secret in fortune making. All you do is buy cheap and sell dear, act with thrift and shrewdness, and be persistent."
—Hetty Green

Hetty Green, circa 1897
Library of Congress

Hetty's Interview: Part II

I was born on November 21, 1834, in New Bedford, Massachusetts—the firstborn child of wealthy New England Quaker parents, Edward Mott Robinson and Abby Howland. In addition to being born into wealth, I was also born into colonial royalty. My mother was a descendant of Henry Howland—a brother of Mayflower passenger John Howland. Although I was a beautiful and healthy baby, my parents' hope for a son had been dashed. Within nine months, my mother's belly began to grow big again, and their dream of having a son came true when my brother, Isaac, was born. Unfortunately, their dream of having a male heir was short-lived—Isaac died a few weeks after being born. My mother, no doubt fearing my father's anger, never recovered from the loss. My mother took to her bed with chronic melancholia after the death of my brother.

When I was about two years old, my father sent me to live with my Aunt Sylvia and Grandfather Gideon. Looking back, I believe my mother's mental state interfered with her ability to care for me. Regardless of the reasons, the pain of being sent away and feeling rejected by my parents followed me for the rest of my life.

The relationship I had with my fun-loving grandfather was my saving grace. I blossomed into an intelligent and spirited child under his care. When his eyesight began to fail, I read the commerce section of the local paper to him, which contained stock and commodity quotes. During this time together, he taught me how to make wise investment decisions by interpreting financial numbers.

At age ten, I entered Eliza Wing's (a Quaker) boarding school in Sandwich, Massachusetts. My father told me it was for my own good, so I wouldn't be spoiled. Once again, I began to feel rejected by my family. I arrived to find a miserly state of existence. There were no generous meals, pretty clothes, or comfortable rooms. The clothes provided to me were worn and plain. Small portions of the poorest quality and tasteless food were the norm. At my grandfather's house, I was given rich, creamy milk to drink as well as gobs of butter to spread on my bread. During my stay at the boarding school, I was provided with skim milk and bread without butter. My impoverished existence was ruled by Quaker discipline, physical chores, school lessons, and Bible scriptures.

At the age of fifteen, I attended a summer session at Friends Academy, followed by three years at Anna Cabot Lowell's finishing school in Boston. As part of my preparatory education, my father enrolled me in dance lessons at Lorenzo Papanti's Dance Studio, where I learned the proper behavior and courtly grace required of socialites when attending dances or balls. I was older than most girls when I made my debut in polite society. Most debutantes I was presented alongside ranged in age from sixteen to eighteen years old—I was nineteen. I suppose my father was trying to help me find a suitable husband, but it failed because I was almost thirty-three before I was finally married. After coming out as a debutante, I went to live with my mother's cousin, Henry Grinnell. My father sent me money to buy fashionable new clothes for the upcoming social season; however, I chose to spend a small portion of it on clothes and deposit the rest in my bank account. I stayed with the Grinnell family for only a month before returning to New Bedford, where I began living alternately between my father's house and Aunt Sylvia's house.

My mother remained chronically ill for the rest of her life until she died in February of 1860 at the age of fifty-two. The bulk of her estate went to my father, except for a house she owned, which she left to me. Several months later, my father sold his interest in the whaling fleet and moved to New York, where he became partners with William Tell Coleman. Coleman was a borax miner and pioneer in the settlement of California. He established a steamship line between New York and San Francisco, which would promote commerce and settlement in the area.

On a trip to New York to visit my father, I met the man who would become my husband—Edward Henry Green. He was a native of Bellows Falls, Vermont, but had spent the greatest portion of his early life in Hong Kong and the Philippine Islands, where he became very wealthy. We fell in love and became engaged shortly after we met.

My father died in June, not too long after Edward and I announced our engagement. He left me an estate worth millions, which included a small amount in cash and a warehouse in San Francisco, with the remainder in a trust fund that allowed me to receive income; however, I had no control over the principal. Of course, that didn't sit well with me, but what could I do? It was typical of my father to treat me as an imbecile, no matter how hard I tried to prove myself competent with finances.

About a month later, Aunt Sylvia also died. She had been an invalid for some time, and I was her chief confidant and companion. I was the only heir, so naturally, I expected to inherit her estate. Of course, I was extremely surprised when my aunt—who had never been noted for giving money to charities—made a will filled with public bequests for the distribution of large legacies among her friends and family servants, with her doctor, trustees, and executors being greatly remembered.

I decided to do something about my aunt's will, and with the help of my fiancé, I challenged it in court. I provided the court with the will Aunt Sylvia made, which left the entire estate to me. It also included a clause that invalidated any subsequent wills. The court questioned the legitimacy of this will and called in a forensic mathematician to determine if the signature was legitimate. The mathematician concluded that the signature was a forgery. What the heck does a mathematician know about signatures? I wonder how much money the trustees paid this scoundrel to get him to testify against me. They won the case with their false testimonies. First of all, they said the relationship between me and my Aunt Sylvia had not been close enough for her to have left me her estate and that the signature on the will I provided was a forgery because it included a clause that invalidated any subsequent wills. Bunch of thieves, they are, and they are paying for it on this side of the veil!

My father stipulated in his will that whoever married me could not touch my money, which was to be free from the debts, control, or interference of any such husband. Before I married Edward, I made him sign a prenuptial agreement stipulating that he had no right to my money, both present and future. The agreement also stated that I would never be liable for any of his debts or obligations, nor would I be responsible for any of his joint expenses. Soon after getting married, we moved to London, partly because some of my cousins were trying to have me indicted for forgery. During our time there, we had two children—Edward, whom we called Ned, and Sylvia, whom I named after my Aunt Sylvia. We stayed in London for seven years before returning to Edward's family home in Bellow Falls. Around 1874, I devoted myself to creating my fortune. I purchased government bonds, railroad stocks, mortgages, and real estate in New York, Chicago, Kansas City, St. Louis, San Francisco, and Texas. I also maintained a fund for lending purposes.

My husband lost his fortune through speculation in the stock market. There were also reports of his philandering. My husband loved a good time, and I could tolerate most of his philandering; however, the one thing I couldn't tolerate was his thievery. I used my money willingly once before to get Henry out of a speculative bind he put himself into, which I wasn't happy about. But the straw that broke the camel's back occurred when my bank used my money to cover his speculative losses without my consent. Neither the bank nor Edward showed regard for me as the rightful owner of my money. After that, I packed up my bags and brought my two children with me to New York, leaving Edward Henry Green behind. Although we remained separated, we never officially divorced. I loved Henry, and so did our children, but I couldn't allow myself to be a victim of his recklessness. I made sure he had a comfortable lifestyle for the rest of his life. I eventually converted to the Episcopalian faith so I could be buried alongside him one day.

The newspapers loved making money at my expense, so it's no wonder that I was constantly in the limelight. There were always headlines about me, but nothing bothered me more than the articles that accused me of neglecting my son. Ned injured his leg during a sleighing accident when he was nine years old. It healed; however, it left him with a deformity that caused him considerable discomfort later on as a young adult. He was a big man—over six feet tall—and his limp got worse. I knew the only relief would be for the surgeon to take his leg. I loved my children far more than silver and gold. They both attended parochial schools, and no expense was ever spared for them. Ned attended Fordham College in the Bronx and studied law in Chicago. Afterward, he went to work for me, managing our real-estate holdings in Chicago and then on to Texas, where he acted as my purchasing agent on the Texas & Midland Railroad. He eventually became president of my line and moved to Texas permanently.

Sylvia lived with me until her thirties because most of her suitors were just after her fortune. I disapproved of all of them except for Matthew Astor Wilks. She courted him for two years before they were married. Matthew was the great-grandson of John Jacob Astor (America's first millionaire). He entered the marriage with two million dollars of his own wealth. Nevertheless, I made him sign a prenuptial agreement waiving his right to inherit any of Sylvia's wealth. After Ned and Sylvia left home, I frequently moved among hotels and boarding houses in Brooklyn, New York, and New Jersey, mainly so I could avoid New York's property tax. I was New York's largest lender, so I figured I didn't need to contribute a penny more.

After suffering several strokes, I died on July 3, 1916. I left behind an estate with a value of about one hundred million dollars. My estate was split between Ned and Sylvia, who I'm sure enjoyed the money substantially more than I did. Ned joined me in heaven several years later. He died from heart disease. I was relieved that he left his money to his sister instead of his wife, Mabel, to squander. Neither of my children had children of their own, so the inheritance Ned left to Sylvia was bequeathed to different charities upon her death. Although I didn't care much for Mabel, I wished she and Ned could have had children of their own to leave an inheritance to. I had wished the same for Matthew and Sylvia; however, I am sure the money Sylvia left for various charities went to good use.

~ 4 ~

SHEDDING LIGHT ON THE MISERLY HETTY

"American women would be much happier if they learned the principles of business in girlhood."
—Hetty Green

Hetty & her Skye Terrier circa 1900
Wikimedia Commons

During the interview, I found Hetty Green to be assertive and kind, with no attempts to manipulate my perception of her true personality. In her earthly life, she filled the roles of wife, mother, daughter, friend, businesswoman, and stealthy philanthropist. Although it's not necessary to be a psychic to form a subjective opinion of Hetty Green, it's impossible to give an objective opinion —based on truth—if you're not one. In this chapter, I give my unbiased psychic impression of the different roles Hetty fulfilled in life. The public perceived her as a brain-warped miser. Those closest to her perceived her as some kind of superwoman.

Often referred to as the "*Witch of Wall Street,*" she was misunderstood and constantly maligned by the press. Although she may have resembled a witch dressed in black clothing, she was nothing of the sort. There are two sides to Hetty Green: the public side, which is the unsavory image the media projected about her, and the private side, which is the image people closest to her knew.

Hetty's public image has always been controversial. The press often painted a picture of her as being a miser, but no article was as vicious as the one published in the Sunday, July 23, 1916, edition of the *Richmond Times-Dispatch* entitled: "Hetty Green—Super Woman or Brain Warped Miser?" Just as there are two sides to Hetty, there are two sides to this article. The first part portrays Hetty as a pathological miser who is mentally ill. The second part is much kinder than the first. It portrays her as a superwoman who is a brilliant financial genius. I believe this article is a perfect illustration of how Hetty was perceived both publicly and privately. I feel it's important to understand her true personality to appreciate her business and investing acumen, so, at Hetty's request, I am reprinting this article in its entirety as it was originally printed. (She told me to look for this article before I began writing this section.)

Part I of the Article: The Public Side

Was Mrs. Green, as her friends and admirers insist, a financial genius of surpassing shrewdness and foresight, whose life furnishes an example of honesty that every young man or woman would do well to emulate?

Or was she, as many who have studied her life and character believe, a pitiable monomaniac with a mind so wrecked by insane greed that she dodged her taxes, ignored her duty to her fellow men, and sacrificed even her own happiness in the most miserly way for money's sake?

No man or woman of whom history makes record ever displayed, both in private life and in contact with the rest of the world, a more bewildering complexity of contradictory eccentricities than Hetty Green. To solve the puzzle which she presents to science—to separate her good qualities from her bad ones and form a just estimate of her character—this can only be done by dissecting the mental processes which made her what she was and comparing them with the processes found in normal men and women, as well as those which are known to produce the curious types we call misers.

Like other brain-twisted people, Hetty Green scoffed at the idea that she was a miser and succeeded in convincing many of her friends that it was an injustice to call her one. But consider how she lived—only for money's sake. She gave little to charity and had only a small circle of friends. Her life for many years was given almost exclusively to dodging tax collectors and beggars and to fighting all sorts of legal proceedings. She never used her wealth for the development of great industries, as Rockefeller, Carnegie, James J. Hill, and other wealthy men have done.

Whatever enjoyment she got out of life seems to have been through the accumulation of money and the anticipation that her son might someday be the richest man in the world.

Even death would not relieve her sordid career with a touch of human kindness—her will did not reveal a single bequest to charity. Not only that, but she drew it in such a way as to leave it doubtful whether the state will be able to collect its just dues in the shape of inheritance taxes.

In reply to a Chicago minister who wrote her that she would be lost to Heaven, she insisted on her money from a $50,000 mortgage on his church. "You had better pray for my soul then because I am going to foreclose within thirty days," and she did.

At various times she is charged with having tried to save doctor's bills by applying to free clinics and charitable hospitals for treatment for herself and her family. The loss of her son's leg is said to have been due to such penuriousness.

In little matters, the same spirit was shown. Once, it is said, she quarreled with the washerwoman because she would not reduce the amount of her bill. As a compromise, Mrs. Green ordered that in the future when the woman washed the petticoats she was only to wash the lower half of them. This would enable her to reduce the bill!

All these things are to psychology convincing proof of the existence in Mrs. Green of the perverted type of mentality which we call the miser.

One of the first misers of whom we have any knowledge was Dichaeus Dichaenus, a descendent of the Byzantine monarchs, but without any of their extravagances. He carried his miserliness to such an extent that they had not the slightest regard for any human being who did not live and think in terms of avarice. Mrs. Green showed precisely the same symptoms when she repeatedly expressed her admiration for the late Russell Sage, a man of almost if not quite as parsimonious habits as herself.

"The true miser," says Dr. Charles W. Burr, professor of mental diseases at the University of Pennsylvania, "gets pleasure from sensations that give the normal person pain." How well Mrs. Green fitted this description is apparent from even a casual study of her life and habits.

She scrimped and saved on her living expenses not because she had any idea that by living on a more liberal scale she would imperil her fortune, but because like all misers her aesthetic sense was so perverted that she derived a peculiar pleasure not only from the saving of money but from doing all sorts of things which would be revolting to a normal person.

Science has discovered that soon after a miser's brain becomes permanently warped signs of this mental weakness begin to show in his physical appearance. Hetty Green showed all these signs.

Perhaps the most striking of the marks which miserliness sets upon a person's body is to be found in the eyes. Nobody who saw Mrs. Green even once will ever forget those deep-set, narrow eyes of hers. When not furtively roaming from side to side they would fix themselves in a steady gaze that seemed perfectly well able to pierce flesh and bone or a builder's walls.

In Mrs. Green's face long before she reached old age there appeared the peculiar seams and wrinkles which indicate the atrophy of the thyroid, adrenal, and other ductless glands. In misers, these glands shrink and become atrophied in the early stage of the mental disease, and as a result, the miser becomes incapable of normal love, joy, sympathy, and other kindred feelings.

Although miserliness is a rather infrequent mental disease, it belongs to a great class of diseases that are very common. Men and women who can solve the most difficult arithmetical problems with lightning-like speed, but are imbecile or half-witted in other respects, belong to the same general class misers.

But strong as the evidence is that Mrs. Green's brain was warped by disease, the case is not proven until we have discovered what caused the malady. As Professor Freud, the great Austrian scientist, and other scholars have shown, misers are made, not born. The mental weakness which they develop is either the result of some unfulfilled longing or some hidden pent-up memory.

Hetty Green's obsession and delusion which burnt away all normal human feeling and put in its place the most sordid kind of miserliness can undoubtedly be ascribed to the strife following her father's death. It was the long series of lawsuits that nearly robbed her of her heritage that embittered her and warped and twisted her brain out of all normal shape.

Psychology does not attempt to deny that Hetty Green possessed extraordinary ability and that her intentions were undoubtedly the best. What it does insist on is that wealth has become a monomania with her and that as this mental disease progressed it made her view herself and her relations to the world in an abnormal light. Her great talents were wasted in the futile effort to make the actualities of life conform to her insane viewpoint.

Part II of the Article: The Private Side

Convincing as the evidence that the late Mrs. Hetty Green was a "brain-warped miser" may be to psychologists, it will have no weight to those who knew her intimately either in business, socially, or through her numerous charities. To them, she will ever remain one of the world's super-women, a brilliant financial genius of whom America may well be proud, and one whose life furnishes an inspiring example to future generations.

In business efficiency, Mrs. Green's friends say, there are few captains of industry to be compared with her. Until almost the day of her death, she personally directed the multifarious details of business enterprises that extended into every part of the country and yielded an annual profit of over $5,000,000. And she did it in a little office not more than ten feet square, and with the assistance of only a clerk, a typewriter girl, and an office boy.

Her ability as a manipulator of large investments is proverbial in the world's financial centers, where for years she operated with phenomenal success. Her first appearance on Wall Street was made soon after her husband had lost a million dollars there. It took her only a few months to convince the men who had ruined him that she was more than a match for them at their own game.

Just how much Hetty Green's influence often had to do with keeping the country's financial interests on a sound basis and preventing their embarking on wildcat schemes will never be fully known. But it is a matter of history in Wall Street that on more than one occasion her insistence on honest, conservative methods prevented serious disaster.

Once when she had $1,600,000 on deposits in one of Collis P. Huntington's banks, she became convinced that he was using the bank's money in some investments that she regarded as ticklish. She protested to Mr. Huntington in vain. Then she went to the cashier of the bank and demanded every cent she had on deposit right away—and not in checks, but in cash.

The news of Mrs. Green's withdrawal from the Huntington Bank started the rumor that it was going to crash. As a matter of fact, it did have a narrow escape. After that, Mr. Huntington and others like him were more ready to heed Mrs. Green's advice, and they found it of the soundest.

Hetty Green had such a quiet, unostentatious way of accomplishing her financial coups that she won the name of the "gum-shoe financier." She delighted in throwing a veil of secrecy around everything she did, both in business and private life. This applied particularly to her charities.

If there was anything she despised more than lawyers it was the wealthy man or woman who gave not for the mere joy of doing good but for the sake of the publicity they would get. Consequently, she got the reputation of being close-fisted and uncharitable, when she gave away during her lifetime many millions of dollars.

Countess Leary was Mrs. Green's close friend and through her, she made many liberal benefactions of which the world never heard.

From the start of her business career, Hetty Green showed an almost supernatural ability to keep track of the personal affairs of those who owed her money. Many a struggling householder or businessman whose mortgage she held will testify that when he was hard-pressed to raise the interest Mrs. Green granted him a liberal extension of time or lowered the rate of payment. But this was never done except in the case of men who could convince her of their honesty and willingness to work hard. She had no patience with the man who lived beyond his means or the one who was always hunting for "easy money."

In the same way, she kept a close watch on the personal affairs of the hundreds of tenants of the buildings she owned. When ill health overtook them and they were having difficulty in raising the money for their rent and other expenses they would often be pleasantly surprised to find pushed under their door some morning a receipted bill for the month's rent, or, perhaps, a good-sized check. All the little acts of charity were done, as Mrs. Green, herself expressed it, without any fuss or feathers. The recipients often never met face to face the grim-visaged but kind-hearted old woman to whom they owed their financial salvation.

The economics that Hetty Green practiced in her daily life were as badly misunderstood by the public as her charities. She scrimped and saved not for the mere joy of piling up more millions but because she firmly believed that by so doing she was setting the world a good example.

Much of the wrong impression that Hetty Green gave to the world was due to the unshakable strength of her convictions. Once her keen analytical mind had formed an opinion on any subject nothing on earth could turn her from it. It was her firm conviction that the Government was making great wealth pay more than its just share of the State's expenses that caused her to be denounced as an unpatriotic and unscrupulous tax dodger.

"The Bible," said Mrs. Green, a few years before her death, "has been my guide all my life. I lived by it and tried to square my life by the Golden Rule. I dealt squarely and honestly with everybody.

Dorothy Dix, the well-known newspaper writer, who knew Mrs. Green well, was one of the many who believed that when she spoke those words she told the truth.

"Hetty Green," says Dorothy Dix, "was a woman who often gave herself instead of giving money, whose stinginess was an eccentricity, a woman who never gave a beggar a penny, but who during a panic built long rows of houses to give men work. She was a woman of such indomitable strength of mind and body that it seemed impossible that she could die, yet now she has gone where the richest are the poorest. And from my intimate knowledge of her, I know she deserves to fare well on that far journey."

My Psychic Impression of Hetty Green

Growing up, she felt very competitive toward boys, with an innate need to outperform them in everything she did. She maintained this competitive attitude toward men for the rest of her life. As a daughter, she strived continually to show her father and grandfather that she was just as competent at business and money matters as any son her parents could have had.

As a businesswoman, Hetty projected a tough exterior, but inwardly she felt vulnerable, especially to men who envied her and approached her with dubious intentions. This sense of vulnerability caused her to leave her husband; however, it also made her very determined to succeed as a businesswoman. She was a force to be reckoned with and would fight any man both inside and outside the courtroom. She demonstrated to the world that women can stand up against the tyranny of men and beat them in business.

Although Hetty was a loyal and caring wife, the well-being of her children and their financial future were her priorities. After Henry violated the prenuptial agreement for the second time by secretly taking money out of her bank account to cover his losses, she took her two children and left him, vowing never to live with her husband again as a couple. Hetty realized that if her children were going to have the financial future she wanted for them, she would have to take control of the situation. She knew how to draw boundaries with people and did not allow them to cross those boundaries, including her husband. Although she and Henry stayed separated for the rest of their lives, she still couldn't bring herself to divorce him. Hetty lived without the luxuries most wealthy people of her time enjoyed, but she made sure her husband lived in the style he had always been accustomed to.

Henry moved from New York back to his childhood home in Bellows Falls to live out the remainder of his days after succumbing to chronic renal disease. Hetty stayed with him as he approached his final days so she could oversee his care.

Henry was raised as an Episcopalian and, therefore, was buried in an Episcopalian Cemetery with other family members. Sometime after his death, Hetty became an Episcopalian so she could be buried beside her husband.

Hetty had very few friends, but as a friend, she made herself available to lend an ear and sometimes a hand; however, she never blurred the line between friendship and business. Anne Leary was probably the best friend Hetty had, but that didn't stop her from charging Anne prime interest on the $350,000 she loaned her. As a friend, Hetty made many generous, but secret donations to Anne's charitable causes.

If money was Hetty's religion, then frugality would be the one tenet she accomplished with great ease. Unfortunately, the press didn't see it this way. They made her out to be an insane miser instead of a frugal moneymaker. As a Quaker, Hetty was raised to be thrifty—money was a resource not to be wasted on unnecessary luxuries such as ribbons, bows, and lace for dresses. As did all Quaker women before her, Hetty wore unadorned, natural-colored clothing. She was a practical woman who had no patience for the pomp and circumstance of the vain rich. She chose to spend, or not spend, her money any way she saw fit. As a child, she was taught at Friend's school that those less fortunate than her were her equals; therefore, they were entitled to the same God-given resources she enjoyed. So, when she unashamedly sought out medical care for herself and her children at free medical clinics, she truly believed she was entitled to the same free treatment as poor people. Of course, the press didn't see Hetty for who she truly was. Instead, they made her out to be a deranged money hoarder.

I believe Hetty was a stealthy philanthropist. She lived among the poor and secretly helped those who were struggling despite their best efforts. Although she was selective about the recipients of her good graces, she gave to individuals and charitable organizations secretly so she would be honored by God, not man. These were the riches she stored in heaven. She despised pomp and circumstance and believed that those who lived such a vain existence would have a difficult afterlife.

~ 5 ~

THE WEALTH CONSCIOUSNESS OF HETTY GREEN

"For forty years I have had to fight every inch of the way"
—Hetty Green

NY Stock Exchange & Wilks Bldg. 1921
Library of Congress

Hetty's Wealth-Conscious Personality Traits

What made Hetty Green so successful in acquiring massive wealth? What were her personality traits? What thoughts did she have? What behaviors did she exhibit? In this chapter, we will analyze the wealth consciousness of Hetty Green. According to the American Psychological Association, personality refers to individual differences in characteristic patterns of thinking, feeling, and behaving (www.apa.org). It consists of the temperament you're born with, the character you develop, and the conscious and subconscious thought patterns that result from learning and interacting with the world around you. Rich people often share many of the same wealth-conscious personality traits, such as:

- Competitive Mindset

- Desire to Learn

- Determination to Succeed

- Drive/High Energy

- Focus

- Nonconformity

- Patience

- Warm and Fuzzy People Skills

- Persistence

- Risk Tolerance

- Self Confidence

- Strong Intuition

- Work Ethic

Competitive Mindset

Hetty was very competitive. According to the July 20, 1916, edition of *The Lakeland, FL., Evening Telegram,* "She fought from New England through New York, Chicago, and St. Louis to Texas. When somebody wanted to do away with a railroad in Texas, they found Hetty Green on the spot. She redeemed the road, set it going, and won the cheers of the Texans."

Desire to Learn

Hetty always performed due diligence to learn as much about a potential investment as possible before moving forward with it. She kept up with what her competition was doing and stayed abreast of current financial and business news.

Determination to Succeed

From the time she was a child, Hetty was determined to succeed at taking care of her business affairs and making her money grow.

Drive/High Energy

Hetty worked from sunup to sundown Monday through Saturday. Sunday was dedicated to getting caught up on business and financial news, strategizing, and spending time with her children.

Focus

Hetty's whole life revolved around her business affairs and children. She had no other interests, not even social ones. The only pleasure she experienced in life came from activities associated with her business and children.

Nonconformity

Hetty was a non-conformist. She didn't care one iota about the social norms of her time. I'm sure she encountered many instances of men and women insulting her and telling her to stay in her place as a woman; however, she always spoke her mind, and I'm confident she quickly put them in their place!

Patience

Hetty was a value investor. She bought investments such as real estate when the price was low and no one else wanted them and sold them at much higher prices when everyone was crazy to have them. This type of investing takes time and requires a lot of patience.

Warm and Fuzzy People Skills

Hetty had few, if any, warm and fuzzy people skills. She was mostly assertive but could be downright aggressive at times, regardless of the consequences. She knew how to behave appropriately in the social circles of the upper crust, but she hated the pompousness of most rich people and didn't want to socialize with them. She was never one to try and gain cooperation with other people by using polite interpersonal decorum. She was too direct and confrontational for that. Instead, she laid out her demands, and if you didn't agree with the terms, you could go your merry way or challenge her in court. She took no partners because she didn't want to collaborate with others—she wanted to be free to do things her way without any interference.

Persistence

Hetty was persistent in her pursuit to accumulate wealth, and she didn't let anything get in the way—not her husband or her rivals. She started investing the money her father left her long before she left England to return to America. Instead of granting Hetty the money outright, he gave her immediate access to one million, with the rest in a trust, which she had no control over, not even for investing. She left Henry to protect her wealth and the future wealth of her children.

Risk Tolerance

Hetty was a confident investor because she had an in-depth understanding of the financial markets. She balanced risk with reward by spreading her investments among a basket of mortgage-backed loans, bonds, real estate, and railroad stocks.

Self Confidence

Hetty believed that she was more competent at taking care of business than any man she knew, especially her husband. She made business decisions based on her research and never sought out the advice of anyone.

Strong Intuition

Hetty stated in the interview that she used common sense and gut instinct to guide her in all her business dealings.

Work Ethic

Hetty had a diligent work ethic. As previously mentioned, she worked on business matters from sunup to sundown Monday through Saturday. She continued to work until multiple strokes made it impossible for her to attend to business.

Hetty had all of the above personality traits noted in rich people except warm and fuzzy people skills. She was a lone businesswoman who had no partners and formed no alliances. She was taught by her father to owe no one anything, not even kindness.

The Wealth Conscious Behaviors of Hetty Green

As noted in Chapter One, the following thoughts and behaviors are commonly observed among rich people.

Thought #1: Poverty is the root of all evil.

Behavior: Engages in activities to learn how to acquire wealth.

Hetty: She learned early in life that she would someday be responsible for taking care of her financial affairs. She started young by opening and funding her own savings account. She also learned how to read and interpret the financial section of the newspaper and buy stocks and bonds at brokerage houses. After her grandfather died in 1847, Hetty became even more involved in the daily operations of her father's whaling business, including making ship rounds, bookkeeping, inspecting shipments, and negotiating prices with merchants, clearinghouses, and suppliers.

Thought #2: I have the right to be rich.

Behavior: Pursues wealth with great determination.

Hetty: After her Aunt Sylvia died, Hetty challenged Sylvia's will in court by producing a will that was considered a forgery. This would not be the first and last time Hetty challenged others in court. She fought from New England through New York, Chicago, and St. Louis to Texas for her right to be rich.

Thought #3: Rich people are ambitious.

Behavior: Sets goals.

Hetty: Hetty's main goal was to protect and increase the wealth left to her by her father. It was smart to have her husband sign a prenuptial agreement stating that he had no rights to her money, especially with the law of coverture in place at that time, which allowed the husband to assume all rights to his wife's property to do with as he pleased. After the bank allowed her husband, Edward, to access her financial accounts, Hetty took her two children and left him. Although they remained separated, they never divorced.

Thought #4: Entrepreneurship is the fastest way to create wealth.

Behavior: Builds one or more businesses.

Hetty: From her early years, Hetty was in the business of investing and lending. She amassed a fortune as a financier at a time when nearly all major financiers were men. She also owned and operated a railroad line. On December 1, 1892, with the help of her son, Ned, she incorporated the Texas Midland Railroad. The original line—known as the Northeast Extension—was sold at foreclosure on April 22, 1891, and became the Texas Central. Hetty purchased the defunct railroad on October 27, 1892, with the intent to make it profitable and then sell it, which she did on January 27, 1893. I am sure she reaped a nice return on her investment by flipping this line of the railroad!

Thought #5: Money is a resource that must not be wasted.

Behavior: Keeps an accurate record of every penny coming in and going out; may exhibit frugality.

Hetty: From the time she was thirteen, Hetty kept the books for her family's whaling business. As an adult, her business letters were often filled with misspellings, and her handwriting was sometimes illegible, but she had a head for numbers, and her books were always correct down to the penny.

Thought #6: I must have cash on hand so I can take advantage of opportunities when they come knocking.

Behavior: May park cash in money market accounts for quick liquidity, but with higher interest than regular savings accounts, or may arrange for a line of credit.

Hetty: Hetty always maintained cash on deposit so she could easily take advantage of opportunities as they occurred.

Thought #7: I must put my money to work to make more money.

Behavior: Look for investments that will yield the most profit with the least risk.

Hetty: Hetty thoroughly researched all of her investments with the intent of securing the most profitable investment vehicles for the least risk. She also made investments that would give her a continuous stream of income, such as interest from mortgage loans and dividend-paying bonds.

Thought #8: I need to pass my wealth to my loved ones so they will be taken care of and continue to manage the money I leave them.

Behavior: Creates a will and trust for his loved ones.

Hetty: Hetty's father, Edward Robinson, left his wealth to her in a trust account along with a million dollars in cash. Hetty left a will stipulating that her estate be evenly divided between Ned and Sylvia.

Thought #9: For my loved ones to manage the money I leave them, they need financial education.

Behavior: Passes knowledge of wealth creation to children or arranges for them to have a formal financial education.

Hetty: She sent Ned to Fordham University and then to a school in Chicago, where he studied law. After graduating and being admitted to the bar, he became involved in various aspects of his mother's real estate and railroad interests in the Midwest, and in 1892, he moved to Texas at his mother's request to better manage her railroad lines.

Thought #10: I have to take care of my health, so I'll be around to take care of my family and finances.

Behavior: Establishes and maintains good health habits by eating nutritious foods, getting plenty of sleep, and exercising.

Hetty: Hetty avoided sugar and fatty-rich foods, choosing instead to eat plain foods like oatmeal, apples, potatoes, and raw onions. She had a routine of getting a good night's sleep with plenty of activity or exercise during the day, such as walking to and from her office at the Chemical Bank.

Reflections on Hetty's Wealth Consciousness

Except for being warm and fuzzy, Hetty exhibited all of the traits and behaviors of rich people. Even with her tough exterior, there was a soft and caring side to Hetty that most people of her time and ours are unaware of. She cared about average working-class people. While living in modest boardinghouses, it was reported that Hetty often nursed ill neighbors throughout the night and was known for handing out piggy banks containing money to children with admonitions to save. As stated in the last chapter, I believe Hetty was a stealthy philanthropist. She lived among the poor and secretly helped those who were struggling despite their best efforts. Although she was selective about the recipients of her good graces, she gave to individuals and charitable organizations secretly so she would be honored by God, not man. These were the riches she stored in heaven. She despised pomp and circumstance and believed that those who lived such a vain existence would have a difficult afterlife.

Despite her groundbreaking position as a woman in finance, Hetty never admitted to being a feminist. When asked, she refused to advocate for the right of women to vote, stating that she had enough to do to take care of her own affairs and that other women should learn to do the same. She was a conventional mother who raised her children with traditional values. It was Ned whom she trained to take over business operations while keeping her daughter, Sylvia, as a companion until she was married.

Although Hetty has historically been ridiculed for her oddities, she has always been respected for her financial knowledge and power. During the financial panic of 1907, when New York City was so low on funds that it froze the hiring of new police officers and municipal construction projects, Hetty's loan of $1.1 million helped keep the government running. This wasn't the first time she bailed New York out. She made similar loans to the city in 1898 and 1901.

Achievement in business brought her the kind of happiness that spending her fortune could not. She proved herself more than the equal of any man, and she did it on her own terms. Hetty didn't live by others' rules or expectations. Had a man demonstrated such a monomaniacal zeal for acquiring wealth, no one would have seen him as odd or peculiar. Hetty was extremely frugal; therefore, many people perceived her as being a pathological miser, but in her mind, she was maximizing the amount of money she could put to work. Many people of her time believed she didn't allow herself to enjoy her money, but that's not true. What they don't understand is that she derived her joy from making money rather than spending it. Hetty's life was an obsessive quest to prove that she could manage the family fortune as well as, if not better than, any man. Over the years, her own investments multiplied and vastly outperformed the funds left in her trust, which she finally gained control of in 1896 upon the death of the last trustee. Anyone who has ever called her a pathological miser could definitely benefit from her timeless wisdom.

~ 6 ~

THE COMMODORE'S INTERVIEW

"I have been insane on the subject of money-making all my life."
—Cornelius Vanderbilt

Cornelius Vanderbilt
Library of Congress

The Commodore's Interview: Part I

I first encountered Mr. Cornelius Vanderbilt many years ago while self-touring the beautiful Biltmore Mansion in Asheville, North Carolina. He followed me around and talked about how he was disappointed with his grandsons, especially George Washington Vanderbilt II. He said, "All my grandsons are idiots. They threw away the fortune I left them with their wasteful extravagance and lack of business sense. They were all a bunch of incompetent, stupid asses. None of them deserves the empire Billy and I left them. George is especially stupid because he wasted money on a castle built amongst the cemeteries with dead people inside and out. I guess that makes it just another mausoleum!" I responded to Mr. Vanderbilt by telling him I thought the "castle" was a magnificent work of architecture surrounded by beautiful gardens, and I was happy to be touring such a wonderful place. He replied by saying, "Lady, you don't know what you're talking about."

He changed the subject and started talking about how he liked me because I was a genuine medium, not like Victoria Woodhull, who was a charlatan. He said he put up with Victoria because she had good connections, and he loved her beautiful sister, Tennessee.

Because Cornelius made contact with me at the Biltmore Mansion, I felt that I would easily be able to reconnect with him again for an interview. I called out to him, and sure enough, he appeared to me and said, "Well, it's the medium from George's palace. I take it you want to talk to me." I told him that I was writing a book and wanted to tell his story. He said, "Sure, I think I have a lot of important things to say, and I'll do anything for a pretty lady like you." So, without further ado, we begin.

Q: Mr. Vanderbilt, Thank you for agreeing to be interviewed.

A: You are mightily welcome, Madame; you may call me *Commodore*. As pretty as you are, you can call me anything you like, just as long as you call me!

Q: Thank you; I will call you *Commodore*. Why were you so driven to succeed in business?

A: As a young man, I discovered that I had what it takes to be successful in business—it just came naturally. I learned most of what I needed to know about the steamboat business from Mr. Gibbons. He was both a father figure and a mentor to me. I became involved in every aspect of his business. He eventually appointed me as his general manager. As such, I became involved in his legal battle to fight the monopoly given to Aaron Ogden by the state of New York. The Supreme Court decided the federal government has authority over commerce, not the states. Mr. Ogden's monopoly over the Hudson was dissolved, and we could expand our business.

Business excites and thrills me. For as long as I can remember, I have loved every part of it. I knew I could make transportation better for everybody, especially the common man, and I did—that's why I'm driven!

Q: Did any of your children participate in the business?

A: Billy was the only one to work in the business, which was a miracle. Billy was a late bloomer. It took a long time for him to get a business backbone. The only son who showed any real promise of succeeding in business was my youngest son, George Washington. Unfortunately, he died from that damn consumption shortly after returning from the war of the rebellion. Up until that time, my two other sons, Billy and Jeremiah, showed no motivation for business. They were downright lazy and slow to learn!

Q: Did any of your sons-in-law participate in the business?

A: Horace, Maria's husband, helped me out with special tasks, such as legal and banking projects. He also acted as a consultant regarding the railroads. He was a very helpful and dedicated son-in-law.

He was the most helpful one out of all my sons-in-law. Daniel Allen helped me with the Accessory Transit Company. I guess I was lucky to have such talented sons-in-law.

Q: Did any of your grandchildren participate in the business?

A: Billy's four sons helped him carry out certain duties, but they were never really in charge of anything. After Billy died, they managed to destroy the Vanderbilt empire. They were nothing but a bunch of lazy, incompetent, lousy spendthrift idiots. They had none of the business sense Billy and I had.

Q: I'm sure you don't mean that. Certainly, they have other admirable qualities, such as an appreciation for cultural things like art and books.

A: Nay, business is the only thing that matters! Ya can't make money on cultural things!

Q: From what I understand, Billy had a great appreciation for art and its monetary value, and he turned out to be a great businessman. Are you aware that he doubled the inheritance you left him?

A: Yes, I am very pleased. I told him just before I died to keep the money together, and he did. It was his sons who let the money go. Their spendthrift ways were the first mistake in a long line of mistakes. Although I could have purchased a palace far finer than William's son, George, I was frugal with my money, so there would be plenty available for opportunity when it appeared. Their spendthrift ways and poor business decisions led to increasing losses over the decades.

Q: Many businesses experience large losses at one time or another. What was the biggest loss you had to endure?

A: Well, ma'am, that would be the Erie debacle.

Q: Why?

A: Daniel Drew, Jim Fisk, and Jay Gould watered-down shares of the Erie Railroad by issuing fraudulent stock to keep me from rescuing the railroad. Out of fear that I would go after him, Drew gave me some of my money back. I was also able to get some money for my shares on the London Exchange. It was Erie's other stockholders who were hurt the most. The value of their shares was diluted by 50%. I never liked any of these sorry rascals. They were all thugs and deserved to go to jail for their criminal acts. They ended up with the railroad and drove it to destruction. They looted it until there was nothing left to loot.

Q: It's my understanding that instead of suing the men who attempted to steal the Nicaragua line, you chose to run them out of business. Why did you take this action?

A: I knew I could cause them more harm and do the public a lot of good by running them out of business instead of going before a judge who might be bought.

Q: What do you mean by *bought*?

A: I mean a corrupt judge that can be bribed.

Q: Did you ever manipulate stock?

A: No, I never traded stock in a detrimental way to the public. I only traded in a way that would benefit a business and improve it. For instance, when everyone else was dumping the stock of a competitor's business, I would buy enough shares to gain a controlling interest, then I would drive it to profitability by providing superior service at a lower price. The company and its stockholders always benefited when I took over.

When the Jay Cooke Bank went bankrupt in 1873, I called a meeting with some of my wealthy allies in town to see what we could do to prevent a market collapse. We all agreed to help prop up the market by buying stock when the exchange opened the next day. Well, it worked for the first day, but stocks crashed the day after. The exchange closed and didn't reopen for ten days. So, if I did anything to influence the market, it was because I wanted to help.

Daniel Drew, Jim Fisk, and Jay Gould were the manipulators on Wall Street—damn scum of the earth they were! They destroyed everything and everybody in their path!

Q: What prompted you to scale back the steamboat business and become involved in the railroad business?

A: Billy brought it to my attention that the railroads were taking a good deal of transport business away from the steamers. He asked me to consider scaling back on the steamboat fleet and began buying up railroads. I thought it was a good idea, so I put him in charge of getting as much information as possible about the railroad business. Soon after, we acquired the New York and Harlem lines, followed by the Hudson and New York Central lines. Billy worked under my direction during the acquisitions; however, he did such a fine job that I eventually allowed him to take over the whole operation under my watchful eye.

Q: How did you acquire your railroad holdings?

A: Well, I started by buying up shares in the Stony (Stonington) until I had a controlling interest and was voted in as president. After serving as President, I decided I had what it takes to make the railroad business profitable, so after I completed the Nicaragua project, I turned my attention to buying up stock in Harlem. I took it over and made it profitable. They called it cornering; I called it being a good Samaritan. Next, I took control of the Hudson, New

York Central, Lake Shore & Michigan, and Canada Southern. I consolidated the New York Central and Hudson and worked to connect many of the lines to other lines to extend service.

Q: How do you know if someone has what it takes to be successful in business?

A: They will behave in a certain way.

Q: How will they behave?

A: Well, let's see. They'll show motivation for something great. They have certain ideas in mind and work towards accomplishing them. Like my son George. He showed great promise and would have made a fine businessman. He was very smart and a natural leader. You might already know that he was a captain in the military. He would have inherited my business if he had survived me.

Q: These days, we call what you're referring to as goal setting. What other traits might they exhibit?

A: They will have the ability to think about ways to come out on top and come up with a plan to do so.

Q: This is what we refer to in the twenty-first century as strategic planning. What else must they demonstrate?

A: They must have the desire to stay the course until they come out on top.

Q: My generation refers to this trait as passion. Is there anything else?

A: Yes, they will want to learn everything they can about the business they're pursuing, either by reading everything they can find or getting someone to mentor them.

Q: What did you enjoy most about business?

A: I enjoyed it all, from beginning to end, but the thing I loved most was beating out the competition by providing superior service and accommodations at a lower price. I loved driving the greedy sons-a-bitches out of business!

Q: Is it true that you believed in Spiritualism?

A: I didn't practice Spiritualism, but I was fascinated with the possibility of communicating with my family, especially my son George. I consulted with Mrs. Tufts on Staten Island many times. My mother and son, George, came through often. There were things she knew that she couldn't possibly have known if the spirits hadn't told her—very personal things! She also knew I was being haunted by spirits. These specters haunted my dreams and even manifested to me in my house and office. It took a little while, but she was able to get rid of them.

Q: Did you ever rely on spirits for business advice?

A: I asked the spirits for insight into my business dealings from time to time, not to tell me what to do but to validate certain things I wanted to know.

Q: Did you ever ask the spirits for investing tips?

A: Mrs. Tufts never gave me investing tips from spirits, but Victoria did. I didn't ask her for advice on investing; she just offered it, saying it was from my mother. Well, a good deal of it panned out, but a lot of it didn't. Like I said before, she was a charlatan and the lowest form of life!

Q: You apparently don't like Victoria. Why not?

A: After all I did for her, she put a knife in my back and turned it with her venomous speeches against me. She's a damn ungrateful vixen!

Q: Did you rely on gut instinct when making business decisions?

A: What do you mean by *gut instinct*?

Q: What I mean is, did you ever rely on the feelings in your gut when making business decisions as to whether or not to proceed in a certain way?

A: Oh, I always looked at a business situation from all angles before I made a decision; then, I knew in my gut what I needed to do.

Q: If you could do it all over again, what would you do differently?

A: The only thing I would do differently is marry a pretty woman who loves sex. I tried to marry Tennie, but she wouldn't have me. She was pretty, young, and she liked to please me!

Q: Are you trying to make me blush?

A: Madame, I'd like to do more than that!

Q: Commodore, you are incorrigible! Once again, I want to thank you for the interview. Is there any advice you would like to give that might be beneficial to someone engaged in operating their own business?

A: Sure, anyone engaging in business must have a winning mindset. They must be constantly thinking about ways to come out on top and win at the game of business. Money is just a trophy for a job well done. You know you've done your best to serve your customers when you're still in business and your competitors are out!

Thank you, Cornelius. This concludes the first part of our interview. In the second part, I would like you to tell your life story. We'll do that in a day or so after we have had sufficient time to rest and recharge our batteries.

~ 7 ~

THE COMMODORE TELLS HIS STORY

"The lack of money is the root of all evil."

—Cornelius Vanderbilt

North Star circa 1900
Bain News Service, Library of Congress

The Commodore's Interview: Part II

My Life Growing up as a Boy in Business

I was born near Stapleton, Staten Island, New York, on May 27, 1794, to Cornelius and Phebe Vanderbilt. My father was descended from a Dutch immigrant, Jan Aertsen Vanderbilt, who came from Holland in the 1600s and settled on a farm near Brooklyn, New York. My great-grandfather moved to Staten Island in the 1700s and became the owner of a farm near New Dorp. The Vanderbilts continued to live on Staten Island from that time on. My father was a farmer. He made a decent living selling produce up and down the river. I went to school long enough to figure out how to write and do arithmetic. My interest didn't lie in education; it lay in making money.

I spent my childhood helping out on the farm and in my father's ferry business. I carried his produce to market in a boat that he owned. I also carried freight for others, and when the opportunity presented itself, I carried passengers. It was during this time that I made a careful study of the water traffic and transportation lines around New York City. Anyway, my father usually sold the produce in advance; however, he gave me some discretion in the matter of sales. I became a close student of the market and made little ventures of my own with such success that, at the age of sixteen, I decided to buy a boat of my own—a periauger—which was a better boat than my father's. I purchased this boat with my savings, along with the money I earned from clearing eight acres of farmland for my mother.

By the time I was eighteen years old, I owned two boats and was the captain of a third. At the age of twenty-three, I was worth about nine thousand dollars and was the captain of a steamboat at a salary of one thousand dollars per year. I made trips on this boat between New York and Brunswick, New Jersey, where my wife and I kept a small hotel.

By the time I was thirty-five years old, I had established lines from New York to several places on the Hudson River and Long

Island Sound to carry freight and passengers. I built boats according to plans that were largely my own. These boats were the very best of their class regarding speed, comfort, and capacity. I demanded excellence in the work of my employees and always rewarded those who were faithful and efficient. I wasted no time in firing employees who did not render effective service.

When I was forty-five years old, I had a net worth of about five hundred thousand dollars. I had such an extensive line of vessels that I became known as *The Commodore*. During this time, I disposed of my Hudson River interests and devoted myself to extending and improving the traffic on Long Island Sound.

In the California gold rush, there was widespread excitement, and thousands of people were eager to reach California as soon as possible; however, transportation was hard to get. I took advantage of this opportunity and immediately established a line of steamers on the Nicaragua route to San Francisco. This venture was successful and made me very large profits. Later on, I established a line between New York and Havre.

I sold my Nicaragua line on what I believed were very advantageous terms. Determined to take a vacation—after having worked for more than forty years without rest or vacations—I built a steam yacht that surpassed any other at the time, both in size and equipment. I called this vessel the North Star, and in it, I took my family and a party of friends for a long pleasure trip to the Old World.

On returning to America, I discovered that those to whom I had sold the Nicaragua line were trying to cheat me out of making the payments they agreed upon. Most men would have sought justice in the courts, but I was not like most men. Instead of suing them, I established a competing line, and with my great resources and a better understanding of the business, I forced them into bankruptcy. This gave me complete control of a shipping line so valuable that in the next eleven years my profits amounted to over eleven million dollars, making me one of the wealthiest men in America.

When I began to see that the railroads were destined to take a big share of the transportation business from the water traffic on the Hudson River and Long Island Sound, I started quietly buying up shares in the Harlem, New York, and New Haven Railroads. I still had too much invested in steamships to put all of my energies into railroads; however, the outbreak of the Civil War created such a demand for steamships that I was able to dispose of all the vessels I wanted to sell.

The Harlem Railroad had been so mismanaged that, in 1863, its stock was selling for $10 a share. I took advantage of this opportunity to buy a controlling interest in the railroad and, at the same time, bought more shares in the Hudson River Railroad at $75 a share. Later on, I acquired a controlling interest in the Hudson River and the New York Central Railroads and consolidated them in 1869.

Around 1868, I was engaged in a long battle over the Erie Railroad with Daniel Drew, Jay Gould, and James Fisk. I bought up a significant amount of stock in the Erie, which Gould watered down in an attempt to keep me from taking over their mismanaged railroad. Under the threat of litigation, they eventually gave me back most of the seven million dollars they stole from me, but not all of it. I didn't get the Erie, and that's okay, but I did get satisfaction when Gould and Fisk were forced out of the railroad. Drew had already pulled out and had retired by that time.

Once I added the Lake Shore and Michigan Southern Railroads, I was able to offer the first rail service from New York City to Chicago. I became the greatest and most successful railroad manager the world had ever known. I differed from all railroad owners of my time because I improved the roads I bought, bringing them to the highest degree of efficiency, while others like Gould and Fisk made money by wrecking their railroads. I made great improvements in every department of my railroad lines. I made sure the very best equipment and materials were used and that my employees were trustworthy, efficient, and well-trained in customer service. I believe my approach revolutionized railroad management.

Soon after acquiring the Lake Shore and Michigan Southern lines, I began to buy stock in the Central Railroad. Its managers decided to make war upon me and arranged to send as much of their freight and as many of their passengers as possible from Albany to New York by water. This did not prove to be a wise move on their part, for when the ice closed river traffic, I changed the terminus of my railroad from Albany to the other side of the river and refused to receive freight from the Central, which caused the stock of the Central to fall rapidly. Stockholders were eager to sell, and I was soon able to unite the Central with my other lines.

When I was nineteen, much to my parents' chagrin, I married my first cousin, Sophia Johnson. She became a supportive and frugal wife, taking care of our home and bearing us thirteen children, with eleven surviving to adulthood. We lived in a couple of small tenements in New York City after leaving Bellona Hall, where I had a twenty percent stake in operating the inn for Mr. Gibbons. Neither one of the tenements was suitable for my wife and children, so I decided to build my first house on Cornell's lot, which was located on the northeast corner of my ancestral family farm overlooking the bay on Staten Island.

We stayed on the island until 1846, when I moved my family to what would be our permanent home at 10 Washington Place in the Manhattan section of New York City. I had the mansion built to my strict specifications, and it was magnificent, but when it came time to move, Sophia went into hysteria. Huh, women, you just can't figure them out! Please take no offense, my lady. Anyway, I had to send her to an asylum, where she stayed for three months until she recovered and was willing to come home to the new house. It would have been nice for us to continue to live on the island, but I needed to live in Manhattan because that's where my business was located.

I strived to make sure all of my children received at least a fair amount of education, especially my three boys. My eldest son, William Henry—whom I called Billy—was an imbecile growing up. He was slow to learn and showed no promise of accomplishing anything worthwhile. On more than one occasion, I called him names such as fool, blockhead, and blatherskite (someone who talks too much). I didn't mean to hurt the boy; I just expected a lot out of him and wanted him to straighten up. He was a Vanderbilt, by golly, and I wanted him to act like one! It took a while to get him steered toward the right way of thinking. Between me and a business partner of mine—Drew Daniels—we were able to get him on the right track to behaving like someone with some sense. He went to work for Drew at the money brokerage house and learned about that business before coming to work for me on the family farm. He had great success with the farm, making it extremely profitable, so I put him to work in my transportation business. Billy continued to learn the business and demonstrated great competence in the tasks I delegated to him. I left him my empire when I died, and he doubled its value within just a few short years. He turned out to be a truly remarkable man—definitely Vanderbilt stock! I wish I could say the same about his descendants—the ones who lost my fortune. I had such high hopes for all of them, but they turned out to be utter failures in my eyes. They were all a bunch of blockheads—over-educated, over-socialized, over-cultural, over-extravagant spendthrifts—who ended up losing the empire I created.

My second-born son, Cornelius Jeremiah, was my greatest irritation in life. I know he couldn't help being physically weak with fits (he was an epileptic), but he had no excuse for his irascible and indolent behavior. To make matters worse, he was also demanding, extravagant, and fond of the gambling table. His mother doted over him because of his illness, which made it impossible for me to deal with him. I cared about him; I just had no tolerance for a son who would never even try to do well. I always said that no son of mine would have any of my wealth unless he could demonstrate his ability to support himself without my help. Cornelius Jeremiah always wanted my money. One day during the gold rush of 1849, he demanded money from me so he could go to California. I refused to give it to him, so he ran away and shipped before the mast (the quarters of a common sailor) to California. He made it only as far as Cape Horn before finding passage back home, no doubt because of his illness. Anyway, I had him put into an asylum upon his return because he tried to use my name to get money from a bank. He stayed for a short while, and when he was released, I started giving him a moderate allowance to try and keep him out of trouble and keep my name clear.

My third-born son, George Washington, died at the age of four. My fourth-born son, whom I also named George Washington, was the apple of my eye. He was everything I expected in a son—handsome, intelligent, and fiercely independent. He graduated from West Point Military Academy and went on to serve our country in the Civil War. He achieved the rank of captain before being invalided home. I sent him to Nice, France, hoping he would recover from his battle wounds and the consumption, but instead of getting better, he died there. We brought his body home and buried him in the Vanderbilt vault on Staten Island. He was only twenty-four years old, with a promising life ahead of him. I had great plans for him in my business. It deeply saddened me that he would never be the one to take over my empire.

After George's death, I started visiting Mrs. Tufts, my spiritual advisor and medium, regularly. Several of my daughters also patronized her. She knew things she couldn't have possibly known unless I told her. She made contact with my mother and my son, George, on several occasions. My mother also had second sight. Neighbors from all around would come to consult with her on various matters.

Sophia passed away in 1868, and in that same year, Victoria Woodhull moved to New York at the urging of her spirit guide. Mrs. Tufts had retired and moved away from Tompkinsville, so I was in the market for a new advisor and medium. I heard about

Victoria's ability to accurately forecast stocks and communicate with the dead, so I called upon her for a reading. She was able to contact my mother and make several predictions that proved to be accurate within a short amount of time. Her sister, Tennie, was a healer. I often called upon her to provide healing for my aging body. I was immediately smitten by her beauty and began referring to her as my little sparrow. I asked her to marry me; however, she turned down my proposal, so I ended up marrying Frank, a distant cousin of mine. I continued to see Tennie for healing sessions for quite some time after I married Frank.

Although the object of my affection was Tennie, I was initially very impressed by Victoria's psychic powers. While in a trance, she would relay messages from my deceased mother and children. She also told me what stocks would go up or down. While she may have had genuine psychic powers—I can't prove she didn't—her stock tips really came from her friend Josie Mansfield. Josie was a former actress turned prostitute whom Victoria met while acting in San Francisco. Josie was also the mistress of my business rival, Jim Fisk. Anyway, I set Victoria up to become a very rich woman because I would split the profits with her if her tips were right.

In 1869, the stock market crashed (this day came to be known as the first Black Friday). Women were not allowed on the trading floor, so Victoria sat outside in her carriage and sent men in with orders to buy. Both of us came out on top, thanks to a warning from Josie. When people asked me how I was so successful, I told them to do as I do—consult with the spirits. I had a strong relationship with both Tennie and Victoria until Victoria gave a public speech that slandered my good name. Understandably, this angered me, and I withdrew my support from Victoria and Tennie's brokerage firm as well as their paper.

Around 1869, I married Frank Armstrong Crawford, whom I met at Saratoga. She and her mother had fled to New York City to escape the adverse conditions of Mobile, Alabama, after the Civil War. During one of our many walks at Saratoga, I discovered that one of her great-grandfathers was Samuel Hand—a brother of my mother. Frank was a very fine woman—she was tall, pretty, refined, and educated. I knew I had to have her, but I was seventy-five years old and she was thirty. At first, I wasn't sure she would marry an old scoundrel like me, but to my delight, she accepted my proposal, and we eloped to Canada to avoid family interference.

As I expected, our marriage was received with considerable disfavor by my children. They thought they knew what was better for me than I did and that they were entitled to run my life. They murmured amongst themselves about how unnecessary it was for me to take a wife. They accused her of being a gold digger, saying that the only reason she married me was to get my money. I quickly put an end to their crap. I told them they didn't have anything to worry about because I had never planned to give them any inheritance anyway.

When I passed away, I left the bulk of my estate to Billy but made bequests to my wife, daughters, Billy's sons, and Jeremiah. My ghost was present when some of my children challenged the will in court. Suckers! They should have had their hides tanned. I believe I was fair with all of them. I shouldn't have left them anything!

~ 8 ~

SHEDDING LIGHT ON THE MYSTICAL COMMODORE

"When asked how he was so successful, Cornelius replied: 'Do as I do. Consult the Spirits.'"

—Cornelius Vanderbilt

Summoning the Spirits
*George Yost Coffin, 1880;
Library of Congress*

Did the Commodore Consult With Spirits?

Spiritualism—the belief that the living can communicate with the dead—grew in popularity in the 1840s. Séances became commonplace and occurred in private homes as well as spiritualist churches. Mediums—individuals believed to be capable of making contact with the spirit realm—were often sought after to provide guidance in all matters of life.

There were many famous 19th and early 20th-century believers in spiritualism, including First Lady Mary Todd Lincoln, Queen Victoria, writer Arthur Conan Doyle, inventor Thomas Edison, actress Mae West, and Swedish painter Hilma af Klint.

There's been much debate about whether the Commodore consulted with the spirits. Many historians think he was a superstitious man because he didn't have enough education to know better. I don't think that was the case. I happen to know many highly educated people who are believers in the occult. My psychic impression tells me that the Commodore was not just superstitious but a believer in the mystical arts of spiritualism, folk magic, and mesmerism.

It is uncertain when he may have taken up spiritualism. I perceive that it was sometime after his mother's death, but his predilection for it may have been strengthened by the death of George. After the deaths of his mother, Phebe, and son, George, his need to communicate with them drew him frequently to the home of Mrs. Tufts, a medium, in Tompkinsville on Staten Island. Several of Cornelius's daughters, who held beliefs similar to his own, also visited her. Over time, he visited other spiritual workers, including the infamous Victoria Woodhull and Tennessee Claflin, but I feel Mrs. Tufts was his favorite.

I sense he also believed in folk magic. In my mind's eye, I see him having a lock of his hair cut and applied to a poppet—a miniature representation of himself—to bring about his healing through the use of spells cast on the poppet. I suspect he sought this mystical treatment after he was diagnosed with syphilis. I also see him using bowls of salt under his bedposts. I perceive he used salt to prevent nightmares and keep away angry souls whom he hurt in some way.

He also sought other types of alternative healing. I clairvoyantly saw him standing in front of a woman while she scanned his body with her eyes, looking for disease. These days, alternative healers of this sort are called medical intuitives. I also see him lying on a bed while a young woman makes several passes with her hands, sweeping over his body from head to toe. I suppose this could be some form of mesmeric or magnetic healing. This might be Tennie C. I'm seeing. It's no secret that she used magnetic healing to alleviate many of his physical ailments.

On at least one occasion, the Commodore's use of alternative treatments may have caused conflict with his physician. I can see and hear a doctor at his bedside giving him a stern lecture on the ridiculousness of his superstitious treatments. In response, the Commodore shakes his head and waves the doctor away with his hand.

The Commodore had no formal education. He never heard the name Adam Smith. He never studied business, economics, engineering, or advanced math but knew how to amass a great fortune. So, how did he become so rich? I believe the Commodore used a great deal of intuition, along with good old common sense, to help him build his fortune. As reflected in the following quote: "I just knew I could make me a heap of money." I think he intuitively knew he would become rich one day.

~ 9 ~

THE WEALTH CONSCIOUSNESS OF THE COMMODORE

"I have always served the public to the best of my ability. Why? Because, like every other man, it is in my interest to do so."
—Cornelius Vanderbilt

The Great Race for the Western Stakes, circa 1870
Library of Congress

The Wealth-Conscious Personality Traits of Cornelius

What made Cornelius Vanderbilt so successful in acquiring massive wealth? What were his personality traits? What thoughts did he have? What behaviors did he exhibit? In this chapter, we will analyze the wealth consciousness of Cornelius Vanderbilt. As discussed in Chapter One, personality refers to individual differences in characteristic patterns of thinking, feeling, and behaving (www.apa.org). It consists of the temperament you're born with, the character you develop, and the conscious and subconscious thought patterns that result from learning and interacting with the world around you. Rich people often share many of the same personality traits.

Competitive Mindset

Cornelius was very competitive in business. He was customer-oriented and focused his efforts on providing the best experience in transportation at the lowest possible price. Because he was well capitalized, he was able to undercut his competitors' prices to the point where he often put them out of business.

I think the best illustration of his competitive nature occurred when he discovered that those to whom he had sold the Nicaragua line were trying to evade making the payments as agreed upon. Instead of suing the men, he established a competing line, and with his great resources and a better understanding of the business, he forced them into bankruptcy. This gave him complete control of a shipping line so valuable that in the next eleven years, his profits amounted to $11,000,000, making him one of the wealthiest men in America.

Desire to Learn

At a very early period in his career, Cornelius began to carefully study the means of transportation between New York and neighboring ports. He established lines from New York to several places on the Hudson River and Long Island Sound to carry freight and passengers; however, it was during his employment as a ferry captain that he learned everything he could about the steamship business from his employer and mentor, Thomas Gibbons.

Determination to Succeed

Out of his determination to succeed, he intentionally drove his competitors out of business by providing better transportation services for a lot less money. He could be absolutely ruthless when it came to business.

Drive/High Energy

The excitement of business alone was enough to fuel the Commodore's high energy level. With the exception of the North Star cruise, he didn't take long vacations. He enjoyed short stays at Saratoga Springs each year to reflect on business and recharge his batteries.

Focus

Except for the ladies of the night with whom he consorted frequently, the men he did business with, and interactions with his fellow trotters, the Commodore enjoyed little in the way of social life. He chose to focus most of his time and energy on amassing his great fortune.

Nonconformity

Cornelius didn't care for or conform to the social norms of the upper crust. On the rare occasion that he was invited into one of the finer homes of New York's social elite, his undignified behavior usually outraged the hostess. For example, it was reported that he would expectorate his chewing tobacco spittle when and where he felt the urge, regardless of whether a spittoon was available or not.

Patience

He had no patience with employees who failed to provide excellent work and had no qualms about firing them on the spot. Except for his youngest son, George Washington Vanderbilt, he was also impatient with his wife and other children. Cornelius believed George would be the only heir capable of managing his empire. He felt Billy and Jeremiah didn't have the brains or initiative to succeed in business. As fate would have it, George died at the age of 24 in 1863, long before the death of his father in 1877; needless to say, he would not become heir to the Vanderbilt fortune. William became the main heir of Cornelius's empire, which he, surprisingly, doubled before he died in 1885.

While Cornelius could be very impatient with people, he was very patient in business. He understood that certain strategies require time to come to fruition. For instance, when Charles Morgan and Cornelius Garrison—with the help of William Walker—betrayed Cornelius by stealing the Accessory Transit Company, instead of suing them, he vowed to ruin them instead. He formed a rival company to the ATC and managed to put them out of business within two years.

Warm and Fuzzy People Skills

Cornelius had few, if any, warm and fuzzy people skills. He was aggressive, with no regard for anyone who might get in the way of his success. He cared little for the upper crust of society and made no attempts to display proper etiquette or decorum in their presence. Cussing and vulgarity rolled off his tongue with ease.

Persistence

In 1845, the U.S. government offered a subsidy to American steamship lines that would carry mail to and from Europe. This initiative inspired Edward Collins to start the Collins Line, with three ships operating between New York and Liverpool.

Several years later, Cornelius made a public announcement that he was willing to operate a trans-Atlantic steamship line at half Collins's subsidy. Upon hearing the news, Collins told Vanderbilt to accept a subsidy as large as his line because it would be impossible to turn a profit without a large subsidy. Vanderbilt replied, "Then you have gotten into a business that you don't understand."

Congress ignored Vanderbilt's announcement and rejected his offers, choosing to continue the larger payouts to Collins due to rampant cronyism and corruption. Congress went as far as to override a veto by President Franklin Pierce over Cornelius's rejection. Undeterred, Vanderbilt went into business without government subsidies of any kind.

Even without government aid, Vanderbilt and his partners were able to undercut Collins's prices while providing ships that crossed the Atlantic much faster. His persistence paid off. Eventually, Congress had no choice but to terminate Collins's subsidy; and on May 27, 1857, Postmaster General Aaron V. Brown entered into a contract with Cornelius Vanderbilt, Daniel Drew, and Edward N. Dickerson to deliver mail overseas.

Risk Tolerance

Although the Commodore was not afraid to take risks, he took measures to mitigate them. For example, he decreased the risk of competition in his transportation business, both ships and trains, by forming a partnership with his main competitor, Daniel Drew. For seventeen years, they had taken a stake in each other's enterprises in an effort to ensure cooperation instead of competition between them.

Self Confidence

Cornelius was once quoted as saying, "I just knew I could make me a heap of money." This quote alone reflects the confidence he had in himself to become rich.

Strong Intuition

Intuition is a type of knowledge that comes from internal psychic sources rather than external material sources. Cornelius knew exactly what he needed to do to become rich. What he lacked in formal education, he more than made up for with common sense and intuition. There is nothing written about him that substantiates whether or not he was intuitive; however, during our interview, when I asked him if he ever relied on the feelings in his gut to help him make business decisions, he replied, "Oh, I always look at a business situation from all angles before I make a decision, and then I know in my gut what I need to do." This sense of knowing at a gut level is a common form of intuition experienced by many successful people. I think the Commodore believed in the supernatural. He has been quoted as saying to potential investors, "Why don't you do as I always do and consult the spirits?" He also, reportedly, placed salt under his bedposts to ward off evil spirits.

Work Ethic

Cornelius entered into business for himself at the age of 16. In 1810, his mother paid him $100 to clear and plant an 8-acre field. He used the $100 to buy a small two-masted sailboat with a flat bottom—called a *periauger*—which he used to carry freight and passengers between Manhattan and Staten Island. Because he quickly built a reputation for being reliable and charged lower rates than his competitors, he began attracting more commuters than freight. During the War of 1812, Vanderbilt's work reputation resulted in his being awarded an Army contract to supply six posts around New York Bay. He made additional money by bringing food down to New York City from the farms along the Hudson River. He was able to buy two other boats with the profits he made. After the War in 1815, he entered the coastal trade between the Chesapeake Bay and New York, in which he carried oysters, watermelons, whale oil, shad, and many other items. In his spare time, he sold beer, cider, and provisions to ships anchored in the harbor. By 1818, he had saved $9,000 and owned interests in several other boats. He exhibited this work ethic pattern of growing his empire until late in life, when syphilitic dementia made it impossible for him to continue.

The Wealth-Conscious Thoughts & Behaviors of Vanderbilt

Thought #1: Poverty is the root of all evil.

Behavior: Engages in activities to learn how to acquire wealth.

Cornelius: One of his most popular quotes was, "The lack of money is the root of all evil." Another one is: "I have been insane on the subject of money-making all my life." From the time he was a little boy, Cornelius was involved in making money. He carried the produce from his father's farm to market in his father's boat before buying his own; he also carried freight for others, and when the opportunity presented itself, he carried passengers.

Thought #2: I have the right to be rich.

Behavior: Pursues wealth with great determination.

Cornelius: He switched his wealth acquisition strategy from steamships to railroads because he perceived the railroads were destined to interfere seriously with the water traffic on the Hudson River and Long Island Sound, so as early as 1844, he quietly began to buy shares in the New York and New Haven Railroads.

Thought #3: Rich people are ambitious.

Behavior: Sets goals.

Cornelius: After Cornelius took control of the Harlem Railroad in 1863, he later admitted that it was his goal to show that he could take the railroad, which was considered worthless, and make it valuable.

Thought #4: Entrepreneurship is the fastest way to create wealth.

Behavior: Builds one or more businesses.

Cornelius: The Commodore made the bulk of his fortune as an entrepreneur in the transportation industry, first with ships and then trains.

Thought #5: Money is a resource that must not be wasted.

Behavior: Keeps an accurate record of every penny coming in and going out; may exhibit frugality.

Cornelius: He lived well below his means. He loaned but never borrowed money, not even for business. Until the day he died, he never flaunted his wealth.

Thought #6: I must have cash on hand so I can take advantage of opportunities when they come knocking.

Behavior: May park cash in money market accounts for quick liquidity, but with higher interest than regular savings accounts, or may arrange for a line of credit.

Cornelius: He controlled his money by saving and investing it wisely, and he always maintained enough cash to take advantage of opportunities as they occurred.

Thought #7: I must put my money to work to make more money.

Behavior: Look for investments that will yield the most profit with the least risk.

Cornelius: His main money-making efforts went into building a transportation empire. He thoroughly understood this industry and knew how to turn an unprofitable line into a very prosperous one. Many of his competitors, for example, Drew, Gould, and Fisk, who milked the Erie Railroad, didn't reinvest the money necessary to maintain their lines. This poor business practice quickly led to the demise of many railroads. He also invested in the stock or had a partnership interest in the ownership of other companies.

He avoided any type of risky speculation, including commodities and options. Founded by Russell Sage, options started trading in 1872 and were very illiquid, making them highly speculative. The Commodore would have never risked his money in such an illiquid and speculative market. As mentioned earlier, he focused his money-making efforts on the transport business. He also loaned money to other businessmen.

Thought #8: I need to pass my wealth to my loved ones so they will be taken care of and continue to manage the money I leave them.

Behavior: Creates a will and/or trust for his loved ones.

Cornelius: He left an iron-clad will that could not be overturned in court. A few of Cornelius's children, Mary La Bau, Cornelius Jeremiah, and Ethelinda Allen, contested the will in court, which lasted for two years, two months, and four days. Nevertheless, the will was honored as intended. William (Billy) inherited approximately 100 million and retained control of the Commodore's empire, which he doubled in just a few short years. Cornelius left money ranging from $250,000 to $500,00 to each of his nine daughters. His second wife received their New York City home, $500,000 in cash, and 2000 shares of stock in the New York Central Railroad. He left $200,000 in a trust fund for his "sickly son," Cornelius Jeremiah. All four of William's sons received money. Cornelius Vanderbilt II received $5 million. William Kissam, Frederick William, and George Washington each received 2 million.

Thought #9: For my loved ones to manage the money I leave them, they need financial education.

Behavior: Passes knowledge of wealth creation to children or arranges for them to have a formal financial education.

Cornelius: He secured a position at Drew, Robinson & Co. for his son Billy by giving Daniel Drew the use of his speedy new steamship, The C. Vanderbilt, for the People's Line on the Hudson. Drew's firm facilitated long-distance financial transactions by buying notes and bills of exchange from far-removed banks and merchants at a discount, securing payment from the issuer, or reselling them at a profit. Cornelius hoped this job would give Billy a financial education by teaching him the value of money.

Thought #10: I have to take care of my health, so I'll be around to take care of my family and finances.

Behavior: Establishes and maintains good health habits by eating nutritious foods, getting plenty of sleep, and exercising.

Cornelius: It has been said that he was physically active and a light eater all of his life. There is some contradiction as to whether or not he consumed alcohol. My psychic impression tells me he drank ale and gin sweetened with sugar in moderation. I don't believe he ever allowed himself to become inebriated. The only illness that he suffered from was syphilis, which ultimately caused his death.

Reflections on Vanderbilt's Wealth Consciousness

Like Hetty, Cornelius had all the traits and behaviors of most rich people, with the exception of being warm and fuzzy. He was one of the greatest businessmen this country has produced. He had insight into the future of transportation and was a genius at improving existing businesses. His improvements in transportation—both land and water—played a significant role in the industrial development of America.

He embraced new technologies, such as the steamboat and railroad, as well as a new form of business, such as the corporation. He was not afraid to take calculated risks. He learned everything possible about an industry before venturing into business.

He was always in motion. Except for the cruise he took with family and friends to the old world, he never slacked off. He was forward-thinking and futuristic, progressing from sails to steam to railroad transportation. He forged collaborative relationships with others, such as Daniel Drew, who would contribute to his cause, and in return, he would contribute to theirs.

He once stated that he had been insane on the subject of money-making all his life. He knew he would make money if he provided quality transportation at a lower price than his competition. As suggested in the following quote, he always strived to give customers a better deal: "I have always served the public to the best of my ability. Why? Because, like every other man, it is in my interest to do so."

He understood the value of money, which he also hoped to instill in Billy by having him work for Daniel Drew. He controlled his money; he never let money control him. He never lived beyond his means, was never in debt, and never bought on credit. Because Cornelius was better capitalized than other steamboat and railroad operators, he could offer fares that were much lower than those of his competitors, who had banks and bondholders breathing down their necks.

Like Hetty, Cornelius shunned the folly of extravagance. He told his son Billy that any fool can make a fortune, but it takes a man of brains to hold onto it. Apparently, only Cornelius and Billy had enough brains to hold onto the wealth they created. It took just a few generations for the folly of extravagance to topple the House of Vanderbilt. The division of the Vanderbilt fortune in the third generation, accompanied by a decline of family interest in New York Central along with an increase in extravagant spending, began the destruction of Cornelius's empire. No wonder the Commodore followed me around complaining about his "idiot" grandsons as I self-toured Biltmore Estate in Asheville, N.C.

~ 10 ~

J. D. ROCKEFELLER'S INTERVIEW

"I believe in the sacredness of a promise, that a man's word should be as good as his bond, that character—not wealth or power or position—is of supreme worth."
—John D. Rockefeller

John D. Rockefeller, circa 1901
Library of Congress

John's Interview: Part I

Mr. Rockefeller is a very sweet and kind soul. In life, he was a very religious man, so I had my doubts as to whether or not he would respond to my call when I attempted to initiate contact. Much to my surprise, he did, and my interview with him was delightful. As soon as he appeared to me, he told me not to worry about being a medium; he saw the light of Christ around me and knew I was a messenger of God. Throughout the interview, Mr. Rockefeller made me feel at ease with his gentle and gracious manner.

Q: When you were a child, your father, "Big Bill," was on the road most of the time, peddling his remedies. How did your father's way of doing business make you feel?

A: Well, I felt that my father was trying to make a living for us the only way he knew how—by selling his remedies to as many people as possible. I often wished he was home to help out with all the chores that needed to be done. Sometimes he would be on the road for several months at a time, but he always returned with large amounts of money to take care of the charges my mother made at the mercantile.

Q: Did you ever feel that you, your siblings, and your mother were abandoned by your father?

A: Not really; I missed him when he was on the road, but I knew that as long as he was alive, he would be back to take care of us.

Q: How did your father influence your business philosophy?

A: He taught me the importance of producing a quality product and supplying it to as many people as possible. The most important lesson I learned from his style of business is that it is not beneficial to sacrifice family to be in business. My own family was more important to me than anything in this world, and when I had to travel for business, they went with me. I kept homes in the cities where I had major business dealings so I could have a normal family life with them.

Q: Did you feel responsible for taking care of your family in your father's absence?

A: No, I didn't feel solely responsible. My siblings and I all helped with the chores, so nothing fell solely on anyone's shoulders except for our mother. I think she always worried about our future because she was never sure if Bill would come home again.

Q: When you were a kid living and working on the family farm in Oswego, New York, did you ever think you might be a very successful businessman one day?

A: I think I had a natural affinity for business. I was always looking for an opportunity to make money, whether it was by selling potatoes that I had dug up, chicks that I had hatched, or taking a short handyman assignment. During all those years growing up, I never imagined I would have the success I had in business.

Q: How did your mother influence your business philosophy?

A: My mother was a saint! She would always tell me to do unto others as I would have them do unto me. I later learned that was the Golden Rule. People may not believe it, but this rule has served me well. Everything I did in business was to promote business for the greater good of all involved. If others wanted to isolate themselves to their detriment and not work together with the larger group, then that was their decision. There is strength in numbers, and the greater the number of people who join together to make a profit, the greater the profit will be.

Q: Are you referring to the Southern Improvement Company?

A: I'm talking in general, but the Southern Improvement Company is a perfect example of how strength in numbers can create strength in business. The whole industry profited because of our alliance!

Q: Did your religious beliefs ever contradict your business practices?

A: No, why would they? I believed I had a duty to my church and family to provide the very best for them, as God had provided the means, wisdom, and guidance necessary to do so.

Q: Did you ever feel you were being guided by God or intuition in your business dealings?

A: As I said before, I believe God gave me the wisdom and guidance I needed to succeed in all my business dealings.

Q: What were your motivations for the expansion of Standard Oil?

A: To reach and enrich the lives of as many people as possible with our quality product at the most affordable price possible while enjoying the fruits of our labor.

Q: That sounds like a mission statement.

A: Well, we didn't have mission statements in those days, but we did have goals, and we were definitely on a mission.

Q: What did you think about the Sherman Antitrust Act?

A: Well, I guess the Act is okay as far as encouraging competition goes, but it was misapplied to my company. According to the lawmakers, the Sherman Antitrust Act was not created to punish businesses that come to dominate their market passively or on their merit, only those that intentionally dominate the market through misconduct, but that's exactly what they did—they punished us for being successful. We didn't commit any crimes or other misconduct. The growth we experienced came about through good business practice, not surreptitious behavior. We didn't go about growing Standard Oil in an underhanded or sneaky way. We used good old-fashioned common business sense!

Q: Did you feel that the dissolution of Standard Oil into 30 separate independent companies would destroy the viability of Standard Oil?

A: No, But I did feel that the creation of so many individual entities would create an unnecessary administrative burden, which would increase our overall cost of doing business, and—of course—that's what happened. It was the customer who was ultimately hurt by this Act because the higher cost of operating so many companies resulted in higher prices.

Q: How did you feel about the muckraking journalist Ida Tarbell?

A: She was a misguided, venomous woman who was angry because her father failed in business while I succeeded. The other refiners who took stock and joined me and my partners became very rich. Frank Tarbell decided not to, and he was unable to sustain his business. He lacked good judgment as a businessman. He didn't look for an alternative way to prosper.

Q: What kind of things did she write about you and your company?

A: She said that I was a hypocrite regarding my religious beliefs and that the world was worse off because I was in it. She said that my partners and I were ruthless and unethical, and our only aim was to put everybody else out of business. That's just not so; we did what we had to do to survive and grow our business. That's called good business practice. It's not my fault or my partner's fault if others make poor business decisions for themselves. Ida Tarbell was a woman scorned because her father did not make sound business decisions. He refused to join me and the other independent refineries in creating the Southern Improvement Company. We had to form an alliance to stop the overproduction of oil being dumped in the region. This overproduction caused prices to plummet to seriously low levels, which threatened to put everyone out of business. Frank Tarbell couldn't see this. As I said before, he had very poor judgment. I'm sure he was never a good businessman. It wasn't my fault he failed; it was his own! I'm sure Ida Tarbell has figured it out on this side of the veil.

Q: Did you ever allow the business to interfere with family life?

A: I always set aside time for my family. We prayed, played, and went to church together. I worked during the week and spent the weekends with my family unless I had urgent business to conduct out of town. If I had business to conduct for an extended amount of time, I would take my family with me. I ended up buying a house in Mount Pleasant, New York, so my family could be with me when I was there.

Q: Did you ever feel guilty about acquiring so much wealth?

A: Why should I feel guilty? I had a responsibility to my family, partners, shareholders, church, and God. I believe that God provides for us abundantly, but we have to have faith and do our part. I trusted God for my success, and I was amply rewarded. Others must do the same.

Q: Why did you rev up your philanthropic activities towards the end of your life?

A: I wanted to share the bounty that God had provided me with. It brought me much joy to give to others.

Q: Did you ever feel you had to give your wealth away to go to heaven?

A: Of course not; I believe we are saved by grace, not of ourselves or what we may do or fail to do. It is a gift from God. I also believe that heaven can and should be experienced on Earth.

Q: What would you do differently in business or your personal life if you had the opportunity to do it all over again?

A: I wouldn't do anything differently in my business or personal life. I am content and grateful for the life I had on earth.

Q: Are you happy with the relationships you had in your physical life?

A: I am happy with the relationships I forged in my physical life. Those who were at odds with me were not of my doing. I would have preferred to be on friendly terms with everyone, but I can't choose for others.

Q: What traits do you think an individual must have to be successful in business?

A: The successful business owner will demonstrate:

- A passion and motivation for their business.
- An eagerness to learn all they can about their industry.
- A willingness to take a measurable risk.
- The ability to make sound plans for growth and improved customer service.
- Persistence—they never quit or allow failure. They look for alternative solutions to prosper in business.

Q: What advice do you have for individuals just getting started in business?

A: My advice to anyone just getting started in business is to:

- Set and meet progressive goals.
- Value customer and employee input.
- Look for ways to expand your customer base.
- Provide a high-quality product and service.
- Keep an accounting of every penny that comes in and goes out, and be frugal.
- Make department leaders accountable for production and the employees under their charge.
- Always stay calm, because it is only in calmness that you can truly control a situation and make good decisions.
- Keep a daily journal of all business activities that occurred; it will help you recall key decisions or events that happened so you can determine whether or not such activities were efficient.

Q: Thank you, Mr. Rockefeller, for agreeing to do this interview. Is there anything you would like to add?

A: Yes, always strive to be the best at your job no matter what type of work you do for a living; be sure to support your home church and give money, or do charitable work to help your fellow man who is in need; but most of all, have faith in yourself and God.

Thank you, John. This concludes the first part of our interview. In the second part, I would like you to tell your life story. We'll do that in a day or so after we have had sufficient time to rest and recharge our batteries.

~ 11 ~

JOHN TELLS HIS STORY

"I believe that thrift is essential to well-ordered living and that economy is a prime requisite of a sound financial structure, whether in government, business, or personal affairs."
—John D. Rockefeller

Rockefeller with bike, circa 1913
Library of Congress

John's Interview: Part II

I was born July 8, 1839, on a farm in Richford, New York—the second of six children born to William A. and Eliza Davison Rockefeller. Although we had two bedrooms, a living room, and a loft with storage space in the attic, the house seemed small and cramped. The land seemed to go on forever. I remember running through the apple orchard and smelling the sweet, fragrant blooms of the trees in springtime. My father, Big Bill, moved us around several times during my childhood. The first move took us to a farm in Moravia, N.Y., which was a good move because we were close to the Davison Farm, where my mother's family lived. She seemed to be much happier while we were there, but that was not to last. About eight years later, we moved to Oswego, N.Y., where I attended Oswego Academy. I liked the academy; however, we stayed only two years before moving again to Strongsville, Ohio—a town near Cleveland. I attended Central High School there for a couple of years before dropping out to enter Folsom Mercantile College. It was one of the best decisions I made. I completed the course in three months. Soon after, I was able to secure a bookkeeping position with Hewitt & Tuttle, a commission merchant and produce shipper. I also joined and became an active member of the Erie Street Baptist Church, which later became the Euclid Avenue Baptist Church. When I was twenty-one, I became a trustee of the church.

September 8, 1864, was one of the best days of my life because I married my soul mate. Laura Celestia Spelman, "Cettie," was the wife I always dreamed of having. She was beautiful, intelligent, and supportive. She was also a faithful servant of our church. After returning from our honeymoon, I bought a modest house for my bride. We lived there for several years in wedded bliss. Then I bought a much larger house on Euclid Avenue. At the time, it was called Millionaire's Row. Lucy, Laura's sister, moved into the house with us, and when Laura's father died, her mother also moved in. My mother's health was starting to fail her, so we moved her in too. About five years later, I purchased a property with a beautiful view of Lake Erie as an investment and sold it to the Forest Hill Association. They had planned to develop it as a water-cure resort. Their venture failed, so I reacquired it and completed the half-built sanitarium, converting it into what would become our summer home.

Cettie and I had five wonderful children together: Bessie, Alice, Alta, Edith, and John. I loved my family and vowed never to leave them the way my father left us. So, when I began having to make lengthy business trips to New York, I took my family with me. I eventually bought a large brownstone home in Manhattan so Cettie and the children would no longer have to live in hotels—they would have their own home away from home.

We started spending most of the year in Manhattan, returning to our Forest Hills home in Cleveland each summer. No matter where we lived, the church remained the focus of our social life, and our children were taught to give from their own earnings. We belonged to a temperance society, and when they were old enough, we required each of our children to sign pledges of total abstinence from alcohol, tobacco, and profanity. Every day, we prayed and read verses from the Bible together. During this time, we also started taking many family trips to the western U.S. as well as Europe.

Cettie was a certified teacher and loved teaching all of our children when they were young. She gave our girls their early education at home, which included music, art, sewing, needlepoint, etiquette, reading, and arithmetic. John Jr. was the only one to receive a formal education outside the home. Being the only boy in a house full of girls isn't easy for a young man. It was important for him to socialize with other boys and enjoy activities that boys are interested in, such as fishing and hunting. Two of our children went to college. Bessie, the eldest child, attended Vassar College, and John Jr. attended Brown University. All of our children were married by 1901. Bessie hadn't been a mother long before she died, leaving a husband and daughter behind. Laura was never the same after Bessie's untimely death.

Around 1893, I purchased land in Pocantico Hills. The land included houses that we used for our family and staff. We moved into the Parsons-Wentworth House, where we spent winter weekends and parts of each summer and fall. We shared the upstairs rooms with our grown children and in-laws while we waited for the construction of the manor house, Kykuit, to be completed. Due to electrical problems, the Parsons-Wentworth house burned down, so another house on the property—the Kent House—became our temporary residence until Kykuit was completed.

Laura loved Pocantico Hills, and we spent most of our days there. We celebrated our fiftieth anniversary and Laura's seventy-fifth birthday at the Kykuit House with family and a few friends. Unfortunately, she would not be able to enjoy our new home for long. She died of a heart attack while I was away on business in Florida. She had been sick for a long time and was mostly bedridden.

After Laura died, I spent several months each year between *Golf House* in Lakewood and *The Casements* in Ormond Beach. I resided at the Golf house from spring until fall and spent my winters at The Casements. I had hoped to spend winters there until I was at least a hundred years old; however, I didn't quite make it—I died at the age of ninety-seven. They say I died from arteriosclerosis; I just think it was old age. I was buried in Lakeview Cemetery in Cleveland, alongside my beloved Laura. We are together now in heaven, looking as young as we were when we were newlyweds!

During my early days in Cleveland, everyone knew just about everyone else in town. One of my earliest acquaintances was a fellow student by the name of Maurice B. Clark. Little did I know then that someday he would become my first partner in business. When he was twenty, Maurice left a hard life behind in England in search of a better life in America. He landed in Boston without a penny or a friend. It took him three months to earn enough money to get to Cleveland, where he accepted jobs as a handyman. He gained a reputation for providing quality workmanship in the homes of the people who employed him. He continued working as a handyman during the day and went to Folsom's Mercantile School at night. Because he was a frugal man, he was able to save a lot of money quickly.

A few years after graduation, Maurice wanted to establish a business and was in search of a partner. He had two thousand dollars to contribute to the firm and wanted a partner who could furnish an equal amount. I had been working with Hewitt and Tuttle since graduation and was excited about the possibility of working for myself. It was a great thing to be my own employer. Mentally, I swelled with pride at the prospects. Maurice would take care of the buying and selling, and I would take charge of the finance and the books.

Although Maurice was about ten years older than me, he felt like a kindred spirit—we were definitely two of a kind. With the money I had saved and some I borrowed from Big Bill, Maurice and I pooled our money together and went into the produce commission business. We immediately began to do a lot of business dealing in carload lots and cargoes of produce. Our venture was very profitable, and in our first year, we made a lot of money. During the Civil War, we reaped huge profits by selling supplies to the federal government.

Soon after, another Englishman by the name of Samuel Andrews asked us to back him in starting a refinery. We put in four thousand dollars and promised to give more if necessary. Andrews was a genius. He devised new processes, made a better quality of oil, and got larger percentages of refined product from his crude than other refineries of the day.

Around 1863, we entered the oil business as refiners. Together with Andrews, we created and operated the Andrews, Clark, & Rockefeller Co. oil refinery. I sold out my shares of the produce commission business and put all my money into the oil firm of Rockefeller and Andrews. In the same year, we had a disagreement about the management of our oil business and decided to sell the refinery to the partner with the highest bid. I bought the company with a winning bid. Then I brought my brother, William, into the business, along with Samuel Andrews. I renamed the company *Rockefeller and Andrews*.

Sometime later, Henry M. Flagler, who also owned a produce shipping business, partnered with the company. Flagler enticed his wife's uncle, Stephen V. Harkness, to invest. Once again, the company name was changed and became Rockefeller, Andrews, and Flagler. Soon after, the company was refining around thirty-thousand barrels of crude oil a day. We became very prosperous, so we decided to incorporate as Standard Oil Company, Inc. The corporation continued to buy out its competitors, and by 1872, it controlled nearly all the refineries in Cleveland. It acquired pipelines and terminal facilities and vigorously sought to expand its markets in the US and abroad. With continued expansion, Standard Oil refined ninety to ninety-five percent of all oil produced in the US. Unfortunately, In 1911, the US Supreme Court decided that Standard Oil Trust violated the Sherman Antitrust Act and ordered its dissolution. The thirty-eight companies it controlled were separated into individual firms.

From the time I started earning money as a child, I gave a generous amount of my income to the church and charities. I think my desire to give to others grew out of the teachings I received from my mother when I was a young boy. By the time I was twenty-one, I supported my own Baptist Church, other churches of different denominations, and African-American education. God gave me great wealth to enjoy and put to good use, and I was determined to do so. As early as the 1880s, I was receiving thousands of letters a month asking for help. I regularly gathered my family together after breakfast to review the merits of the petitions. Most of these letters were requests for money for personal use, with no other consideration than that the writer would be grateful to have it.

By 1890, I was trying to give here and there as appeals presented themselves. I did due diligence as best I could, almost working myself to the point of a nervous breakdown. It then occurred to me that I needed to organize and approach my attempts at charity the same way I approached my business affairs. It marked an important turning point in my career as a philanthropist. I began to spend less time at the office and more time on charities. It didn't take long for me to realize that I needed to devote even more time to the business of giving, but to do so, I needed to retire from the oil business. So, that's what I did.

I participated in the founding of the University of Chicago by offering six hundred thousand dollars of the first million for the endowment, but only if the remainder was pledged by others within ninety days. The remainder was raised, and the university was incorporated. I continued to contribute for the next twenty years, with the condition that others join me. I gave a farewell gift of $10 million. The total of my contributions to the university was around thirty-five million dollars.

I founded the Rockefeller Institute for Medical Research to discover the causes, manner of prevention, and cure of diseases, and I established the General Education Board for the promotion of education within the United States without the distinction of race, sex, or creed. I also created the Rockefeller Sanitary Commission for the Eradication of Hookworm Disease. Its purpose was to fund a cooperative movement to cure and prevent hookworm disease, which was especially devastating in the southern states. I think my crowning achievement in philanthropy was when I established the Rockefeller Foundation to promote the well-being of mankind throughout the world. Since its inception, the foundation has given assistance to public health, medical education, improved food production, scientific advancement, social research, and the arts all over the world.

It may sound to you like I am some kind of raving egomaniac bragging about all the good deeds I have done. Lord knows, I have certainly received my share of credit for being a robber baron. Everything I accomplished on earth was by the grace of God and His goodness. I lived a life of faith, believing that God rewards us according to our expectations of him. We don't have to wait to get to heaven before we can experience paradise. We can have it right here on earth, but we have to believe we have received it to get it.

~ 12 ~

SHEDDING LIGHT ON THE RELIGIOUS ROCKEFELLER

"I believe in an all-wise and all-loving God, named by whatever name, and that the individual's highest fulfillment, greatest happiness, and widest usefulness are to be found in living in harmony with His will."
—John D. Rockefeller

Playing golf, circa 1932, JDR on the right
Wikimedia Commons

Man of God or a Robber Baron?

My psychic perception of John is that he believed God to be the Source of every good and perfect gift—that abundance was the birthright of every Christian, and that paradise should be experienced on earth as well as in heaven. I believe his motivation to succeed in business was based in part on his sense of stewardship and service to God, his partners, and his fellow man. He tells me that the best thing he did in life was to make Jesus his Savior and Laura Spelman his wife.

He read the Bible and tried to practice its teachings in his everyday life—he tithed, practiced the golden rule, and went to church for prayer meetings with his family at least twice a week. He and Laura taught Bible classes at church and hosted Bible studies at home. They regularly held social events in their home for church members, preachers, and evangelists.

His fellow businessmen had a difficult time understanding why he would give a fortune to Christian groups while trying to borrow millions of dollars to expand the business. From the time he was a small child, he gave to his local Baptist church. As an adult, he expanded his giving to include the poor—black or white—at universities as well as missions and churches in New York City and abroad. As his salary increased, so did his giving. By the time he was 45 years old, he was giving away $100,000 per year; at 53, he started giving away $1,000,000 or more annually. In his 80th year, he happily gave away a whopping $138,000,000. Giving his money away was the fulfillment of the Biblical commandment: "Give, and it shall be given unto you; good measure, pressed down, and shaken together, and running over, shall men give into your bosom." He understood that it is the love of money and not money itself that is the root of all evil, and he loved God much more than money. He knew what the prophet Malachi meant when he said, "Bring the whole tithe into the storehouse and see if I will not throw open the floodgates of heaven and pour out so much blessing that you will not have room enough for it." As illustrated in the following quote, when Rockefeller proclaimed, "God gave me my money," he truly believed it:

> I believe the power to make money is a gift from God—just as are the instincts for art, music, literature, the doctor's talent, and the nurse's, it's yours—to be developed and used to the best of your ability for the good of mankind. Having been endowed with the gift I possess, I believe it is my duty to make money and still more money and to use the money I make for the good of my fellow man according to the dictates of my conscience.

Some historians don't appreciate the way Rockefeller made his money, but few have objected to the way he gave it away. During his life, he gave about $550,000,000 to various charities and causes. He obeyed the commandment of Christ: "Go ye into all the world, and preach the gospel to every creature." His charitable giving helped build schools and churches and supported evangelists and missionaries all over the world.

Healing the sick was also part of his Christian mission. It wasn't state aid but Rockefeller philanthropy that paid teams of scientists who found cures for yellow fever, meningitis, and hookworm. The university-based medical researchers who showed results got more of Rockefeller's funding. Those who didn't produce results were cut off. As stated in the parable of the talents, to him who has, more shall be given, and to him who has not, even that will be taken away from him.

Rockefeller never lost his temper. He was always calm, even in the most difficult times. For example, in 1907, when Judge Landis found Standard Oil of Indiana guilty of taking rebates from the Chicago & Alton Railroad (which was not an illegal thing to do at the time), he fined them $29.2 million. This was the largest corporate fine in history at that time. The British magazine *Railway World* was shocked that Standard Oil Company of Indiana was fined an amount equal to seven or eight times the value of its entire property because its traffic department did not verify the statement of the Alton rate clerk that the six-cent commodity rate on oil had been properly filed with the Interstate Commerce Commission. The New York Times called this decision a bad law and "a manifestation of that spirit of vindictive savagery toward corporations."

It has been said that in the middle of a golf game, a frantic messenger came running through the fairways to deliver the news of Landis's verdict and fine to Rockefeller. Rockefeller remained calm at the news of Landis's verdict, choosing instead to focus on playing golf with friends. He looked at the telegram, put it in his pocket, and said, "Shall we continue, gentlemen?" The verdict and fine assessed by Landis were later reversed in circuit court appeals by Judges Peter S. Grosscup, Francis E. Baker, and W. H. Seaman. Grosscup arraigned Landis for the lower court's decision to convict a corporation that had never been indicted or tried. Unfortunately, Rockefeller was not as lucky in his fight against the Sherman Antitrust Act.

Rockefeller set up the Standard Oil Trust to allow his separately incorporated oil businesses in different states to be efficiently managed by the same board of directors. He didn't set up the trust in an attempt to create a monopoly. Nevertheless, the Supreme Court struck the trust down in 1911 and forced Standard Oil to break up into separate state companies with separate boards of directors. While others panicked, Rockefeller believed that God would pull him through. He did what he could, then turned his problems over to God and tried not to worry. I think the following quote demonstrates his attitude toward letting go of worry and letting God take over:

> I was early taught to work as well as play.

> My life has been one long, happy holiday.
> Full of work and full of play—
> I dropped the worry on the way—
> And God was good to me every day.

This quote by Rockefeller isn't just some religious platitude—he said it because he believed it. The Supreme Court's decision was puzzling to Rockefeller and his partners. The Sherman Antitrust Act was supposed to prevent monopolies and companies "in restraint of trade." Standard Oil had no monopoly and certainly was not restraining trade. Meanwhile, the Russians, with the help of their government, had been gaining ground on Standard Oil in the international oil market. In America, competition in the oil industry was more intense than ever. Over a hundred oil companies—from Associated Oil in California to Gulf Oil in Texas—competed with Standard. Standard's share of the United States and world markets steadily declined from 1900 to 1910, but Rockefeller kept his promise to obey the court's order.

~ 13 ~

THE WEALTH CONSCIOUSNESS OF JOHN D. ROCKEFELLER

"I was early taught to work as well as play.
My life has been one long, happy holiday;
Full of work and full of play;
I dropped the worry on the way;
And God was good to me every day."

—John D. Rockefeller

Next! Standard Oil, circa 1900-1910
Library of Congress

Rockefeller's Wealth-Conscious Personality Traits

What made John D. Rockefeller so successful in business? What were his personality traits? What were his habits? What was he thinking? According to the American Psychological Association, personality refers to individual differences in characteristic patterns of thinking, feeling, and behaving (www.apa.org). It consists of the temperament you're born with, the character you develop, and the conscious and subconscious thought patterns that result from learning and interacting with the world around you. Unlike Hetty and Cornelius, John demonstrated all of the following personality traits associated with wealth consciousness, including warm and fuzzy people skills:

Competitive Mindset

John D. Rockefeller once professed, "Competition is a sin." He believed in an economy of scale and knew everyone could profit if they united together in harmony instead of fighting each other to come out on top. In 1865, the oil industry was just beginning to grow. Most people used oil only for lighting; therefore, the market was limited. Prices became volatile as oil production waxed and waned during this period. Rockefeller and Andrews approached O. H. Payne, owner of the largest oil refinery in Cleveland, to try and stabilize oil prices. They convinced him that by uniting their companies together to have a single oil company operating in northeastern Ohio, they would be able to fix prices and control the production and supply of oil, which often increased or dwindled. Payne agreed, and soon they were able to persuade other Cleveland refineries to join them. Companies that didn't agree to join them were ultimately driven out of business because they were not able to compete with a larger company. A business's size is related to whether it can achieve economies of scale. Larger companies will have more cost savings and higher production levels. Economies of scale are cost advantages companies experience when production becomes efficient. The cost of doing business can be spread over a larger amount of goods, which makes it possible for a company to become more competitive by offering lower prices.

Rockefeller has often been criticized and accused of driving smaller refineries out of business by creating a monopoly. To his critics, including the muckraker Ida Tarbell, he would probably say, *It wasn't I who put them out of business. They did that themselves through the poor decisions they made.* In 1870, Rockefeller united these companies under a new business structure known as a Trust. The newly formed business was called *Standard Oil Company and Trust*.

Desire to Learn

Rockefeller credits his father, Big Bill, with teaching him the practical principles and methods of business. He also learned a lot from working under the supervision of the head bookkeeper at Hewitt & Tuttle, who taught him the clerical work connected with business. He learned all he needed to know about the oil refining process from his partner and chemist, Samuel Andrews. He learned what he needed about business finance from his practical experience working with banks.

Determination to Succeed

John honed his will, training himself to be a master of his emotions, desires, and schedule so he could direct all his effort toward his aims. He set big goals for himself and then attacked them with a disciplined, work ethic. He understood that if you wish to be your own boss, you have to learn how to boss yourself.

Drive/High Energy

From the time he was a little boy, Rockefeller was driven to make money. When he was seven or eight years old, he engaged in his first business enterprise with the assistance of his mother. He acquired some baby turkey chicks, which he found in the wild, brought them home, and fed them milk curds and bread. He took care of them himself, and from five or six chicks, he established a turkey farm containing hundreds of turkeys. He saved the money he earned from various job errands and his turkey business in a little blue china bowl.

Focus

From early boyhood, Rockefeller kept a little book he called Ledger A, which contained his receipts and expenditures as well as an account of the small sums he gave away regularly. Another example of Rockefeller's focus is that he devoted himself exclusively to the oil business and its products. The company never went into outside ventures but kept to the enormous task of perfecting its core organization.

Nonconformity

Rockefeller did not conform to the practices of other oil refiners. While other oil refiners in his day concentrated on selling their oil to local markets at the highest price possible, Rockefeller concentrated on making oil affordable to everyone everywhere. Standard Oil rose to power not through unethical business practices, but by providing cheap oil to the general public. Rockefeller told one of his partners, "We must always remember that we are refining oil for the poor man, and he must have it cheap and good." Or, as he put it to another partner, "I hope we can continue to hold out with the best illuminator in the world at the lowest price."

Unlike his competitors, who dumped the waste by-products of kerosene processing into the river, Rockefeller created other products to sell, which provided additional income and, in turn, lowered the cost of producing kerosene. He passed the cost savings on to the customer.

His competitors complained and condemned him for receiving large rebates from the railroads, but he earned them by supplying large shipments of oil. Without large shipments, he would not have had any leverage to get low shipping rates from the railroads. In any case, those low costs were passed along to consumers by further reducing the price of his oil.

Patience

Rockefeller built his first refinery in 1863. He and his partners continued to grow and acquire refineries, finally incorporating their conglomerate as Standard Oil in 1870. By 1880, they were producing 90 to 95% of the refined oil in the United States. It took patience for Rockefeller and his partners to grow Standard Oil from one refinery to the largest petroleum company in the world, which became Standard Oil Trust.

Warm and Fuzzy People Skills

Rockefeller treated his employees well, and everyone worked together to achieve the company's goals. He routinely praised and encouraged his employees, often referring to them as the *Standard Oil family*. It was not uncommon for him to join them in their work and urge them on. Rockefeller believed in giving his employees praise, rest, and comfort to help them perform their best work. He was kind and soft-spoken with his employees, but also straightforward about his expectations for the quality of their work. He valued their input and often interviewed them on the spot during his factory rounds. He would ask them about their work processes and if there were any difficulties in their production. Of course, he always noted what he learned from his rounds with employees in a journal.

Persistence

Rockefeller once said, "I do not think that there is any other quality so essential to success of any kind as the quality of perseverance. It overcomes almost everything, even nature." When he set a goal, he did what it took to accomplish it. As a teenager, his number one goal in life was to get a job at a respectable business. After attending his 10-week business program, he mapped out a plan for targeting large, successful businesses to apply to. For six weeks, he worked tirelessly to get a job. Even though he faced constant rejection, he still believed in himself. He knew that with persistence, he would get a job.

Risk Tolerance

Rockefeller was very risk-tolerant when it came to borrowing money because he was confident in his ability to be successful as an entrepreneur. Borrowing money to fund start-ups and expansions was the way he financed business needs. Bankers trusted him—his credit history, reputation for business success, and church attendance gave him a high credit rating at the banks, which made it easy for him to borrow.

Strong Intuition

Rockefeller used his gut intuition to forge into uncharted territory. His shrewd, intuitive business sense, based not on his education or work experience as an assistant bookkeeper, helped him become the world's first billionaire.

Work Ethic

Rockefeller frequently burned the midnight oil when he was a young man. Eventually, as business increased and he began tackling bigger problems, he realized this type of work ethic wouldn't be sustainable and could lead him to an early grave. One of Rockefeller's goals was to live to the age of a hundred years so he began to take the opposite approach in the hopes of increasing his longevity. He worked at a leisurely pace, napping daily after lunch and frequently dozing in a lounge chair after dinner. When asked later in life about his extraordinary longevity, he replied, "I'm here because I shirked: I did less work, lived more in the open air, enjoyed sunshine, and exercised."

By the time he reached his mid-thirties, he had a telephone line installed between his house and office, so he could spend a few afternoons each week at home gardening and enjoying the sunshine. Rockefeller mingled work with rest to pace himself, which he believed would improve his productivity. He also believed in the necessity of concentration in increasing productivity and achieving success, as reflected in the following quote: "Do not many of us who fail to achieve big things fail because we lack concentration—the art of concentrating the mind on the thing to be done at the proper time and to the exclusion of everything else?"

Rockefeller's Wealth-Conscious Thoughts & Behaviors

As noted in Chapter 1, many thoughts and behaviors are commonly observed among rich people. John had all of them.

Thought #1: Poverty is the root of all evil.

Behavior: Engages in activities to learn how to acquire wealth.

John: Although he had planned to go to college, he chose at age sixteen to leave high school, which he had nearly completed, and attend a business college in Cleveland. While there, he learned bookkeeping and some of the fundamental principles of commercial transactions. Though it lasted only a few months, this training was very valuable to him.

On September 26, 1855, he went to work for Hewitt & Tuttle, who traded a wide array of commodities on commission. For the next year, he learned the clerical work and details of the business, which would prove valuable to him in the years to come.

His work was done in the firm's main office, and he was almost always present when they talked of their affairs, laid out their plans, and decided upon a course of action. The firm conducted business with many ramifications, so John's education was quite extensive. They owned dwelling houses, warehouses, and buildings that were rented for offices and a variety of other uses, and they made John responsible for collecting the rents. They shipped their produce by rail, canal, and lake. There were many different kinds of negotiations and transactions to which John was exposed.

Thought #2: I have the right to be rich.

Behavior: Pursues wealth with great determination.

John: It has been written that John once exclaimed to an older businessman that he was bound to be rich. He has also been quoted as saying:

"I believe the power to make money is a gift from God. Having been endowed with the gift I possess, I believe it is my duty to make money and still more money and to use the money I make for the good of my fellow man according to the dictates of my conscience."

Thought #3: Rich people are ambitious.

Behavior: Sets goals.

John: Rockefeller was shrewd and ambitious. In 1871, along with Henry Flagler, he formulated the plan for consolidating all oil refining firms into one great organization to eliminate excess production, thereby controlling volatile prices.

They planned for success down to the smallest detail. Nothing was left to chance, nothing was guessed at, and nothing was left uncounted or unmeasured. They used economies of scale in their operations. They built large, high-quality manufacturing facilities and refineries. Frugality was planned into the operation, and nothing was wasted. They owned their own barrel-making (cooperage) plant, white-oak timber, and drying facilities. As a result, they cut the cost of a barrel in half—from about $3.00 to less than $1.50. They owned their own drayage service, consisting of at least 20 wagons and boats on the Hudson and East Rivers to transport their oil. They also owned their own fleet of tank cars. They built huge holding tanks close to their refineries for both storing crude and refined oil. They manufactured their own sulfuric acid (which was used in the purification process) and devised technology to recover it for reuse.

They built their manufacturing plant to handle all the by-products from the refining of kerosene. These by-products were used to manufacture many different types of high-quality petroleum products, such as:

- Lubricating oil, which replaced lard oil as a lubricant for machinery,
- Gasoline, which many refiners in the region secretly dumped into rivers, Standard used to fuel its plant machinery (before the time of automobiles).
- Benzene, which is still used in cleaning fluids and solvents,

- Paraffin, which is still used in candles, waterproof paper, and preservative coatings,
- Petrolatum, which is still used as a base for ointments and medicated wound dressings,
- Naphtha, which is still used as a solvent in dry cleaner solution, varnish, and paint

There's very little written in the literature about whether or not Rockefeller and his partners committed their plans to paper. Regardless, their clandestine schemes, orchestrated in the boardroom, made Standard Oil the giant it was.

Thought #4: Entrepreneurship is the fastest way to create wealth.

Behavior: Builds one or more businesses.

John: In 1859, Rockefeller left his employer, Hewitt & Tuttle, and partnered with M.B. Clark to form his own produce brokerage business. During the American Civil War, he and Clark profited tremendously as they sold supplies to the federal government.

In the early 1860s, they organized a firm to refine and deal in oil. It was Rockefeller's first direct connection with the oil trade. In 1865, the partnership was dissolved. They decided that the cash assets should be collected and the debts paid, but this left the plant to be disposed of. It was suggested that it should go to the highest bidder among them.

Rockefeller had made up his mind that he wanted to go into the oil trade, not as a special partner but actively on a larger scale, with Mr. Andrews, the chemist and manufacturing genius, as a partner in that business. So he arranged a line of credit before the auction for as much money as he could need to win the bid.

At the auction, bidding began at a $500 premium. Little by little, the price went up. Neither side was willing to stop bidding, and the amount gradually rose until it reached $50,000. It advanced to $60,000 and, in slow stages to $70,000. Clark made a bid for $72,000. Without hesitation, Rockefeller bid $72,500. Mr. Clark conceded by declaring, "I'll go no higher, John; the business is yours." Soon after the auction, Rockefeller gave up the produce firm of Clark & Rockefeller by having Clark take over the business.

Thought #5: Money is a resource that must not be wasted.

Behavior: Keeps an accurate record of every penny coming in and going out; may exhibit frugality.

John: As a young man, he began keeping a little red journal he called Ledger A. In this journal, he kept a strict accounting of his income and expenses. This behavior demonstrated his reverence for the value of money earned and the accumulative power of every cent.

As a child, John learned the value of thrift. Nothing was wasted; even table scraps were recycled as fertilizer in the gardens. He applied the same principle of thrift to his refining business by selling the by-products of kerosene production. Throughout the 1870s, Standard Oil developed over 300 petroleum-based products for consumers.

Oil-based paints were produced and sold directly to consumers, as well as a base for paint manufacturers; paraffin wax, which was less expensive than beeswax, was sold to candle makers; petroleum jelly was produced and used for a variety of purposes; and the tar from sludge was sold to paving and roofing suppliers. Chewing gum also became a product line. When Rockefeller saw the price of wooden barrels go up, he cut off his suppliers, purchased raw lumber, and hired coopers to build his own barrels, thereby reducing the cost to make each barrel from a little over two dollars to less than one. Rather than hiring third-party pipefitters and plumbers, he employed his own, paying them an hourly wage rather than a set fee for a particular job.

Thought #6: I must have money on hand so I can take advantage of opportunities when they come knocking.

Behavior: May park cash in money market accounts for quick liquidity, but with higher interest than regular savings accounts, or may arrange for a line of credit.

John: He never used his own money for start-ups or expansions, mainly because he didn't have it. He borrowed money from his father to start his first business with Clark. He borrowed money from banks to expand that business. In the early days of Standard Oil, he did a good deal of traveling visiting the refineries, making new connections, and arranging lines of credit to expand the business. It often called for very rapid work, and there was one situation where he had to quickly raise the money for expansion to accommodate the drastic increase in demand for Standard oil. It required many hundreds of thousands of dollars—and in cash. He drove from bank to bank, asking each president or cashier, whomever he could find first, to be prepared to give him all the funds they could loan him. He told them he would be back to get the money a little later. He rounded up all of the banks in the city and kept going until he had secured the necessary amount.

Thought #7: I must put my money to work to make more money.

Behavior: Look for investments that will yield the most profit with the least risk.

John: He invested in the stocks of many different industries, such as mines, steel mills, paper mills, railroads, lumber fields, smelting properties, and a nail factory. He also owned one-third of Standard Oil's dividend-paying stock, which paid out 2/3 of its profits.

It has been said of John that he praised real estate as an investment because "time is on your side" with real estate, and you can hold on to it for as long as you want. John owned timberland and may have sold timber from time to time; however, outside of his many residential properties and other real estate holdings, it doesn't appear that he did any serious speculation in real estate development, but his son did.

John Jr's first real estate investment was Rockefeller Center, one of the greatest projects of the Great Depression era. Construction started in 1931, and the first buildings opened in 1933, with the core of the complex completed by 1939. Rockefeller Center was declared a New York City landmark in 1985 and a National Historic Landmark in 1987.

John didn't speculate on commodities and options. It doesn't appear that he invested in bonds either, although it's possible.

Thought #8: I need to pass my wealth to my loved ones so they will be taken care of and continue to manage the money I leave them.

Behavior: Creates a will and trust for his loved ones.

John: He gave away more than half a billion dollars in carefully chosen philanthropies and transferred $460 million in 1917 to his son, John D. Rockefeller, Jr. He died, leaving a small but very liquid estate.

In 1934, John D. Rockefeller, Jr., set up trusts for his daughter and five sons. These trusts still hold the bulk of his fortune. Another set of trusts was set up in 1952 for his grandchildren. When family members die, their trusts are divided into new trusts for their children.

Thought #9: For my loved ones to manage the money I leave them, they need financial education.

Behavior: Passes knowledge of wealth creation to children or arranges for them to have a formal financial education.

John: He sent his son, John Jr., to Brown University, where he earned a Bachelor of Arts degree in 1897. After graduation, John Jr. joined his father at Standard Oil, where he became a director. Later, he also became a director at J. P. Morgan's U.S. Steel Company, which was formed in 1901. He resigned from both companies in 1910 to pursue his ongoing philanthropic interests.

Thought #10: I have to take care of my health, so I'll be around to take care of my family and finances.

Behavior: Establishes and maintains good health habits by eating nutritious foods, getting plenty of sleep, and exercising.

John: He maintained a lean physique—he got plenty of exercise by riding his bicycle and playing golf, and he ate moderately, avoiding fatty foods and sweets. He never smoked or consumed alcohol. He was well rested—he went to bed at 10:30 p.m. every night and kept a couch in his office and another one in his board room so he could take afternoon naps. He managed stress by maintaining a calm demeanor, regardless of the situation. He loved working in his garden at Forest Hill, which may have helped him alleviate work-related stress.

Reflections on Rockefeller's Wealth Consciousness

John exhibited all of the traits and behaviors of rich people, including warm and fuzzy skills. He was kind, soft-spoken, and encouraging toward his employees. As a schoolboy, Rockefeller once said to a friend as they walked by a rich man's house, "When I grow up, I want to be worth $100,000, and I'm going to be too." This statement demonstrates his determination and faith to become rich. He would work on neighboring farms from morning to night, hoeing potatoes for 37 cents a day. When he was still very young, he had $50 saved, which he loaned to a farmer who employed him. He soon learned he could get as much interest for $50 loaned at seven percent as he could digging potatoes for ten days. Thereafter, he concluded that it was better to let money work for him than to work for money.

In his first position as an assistant bookkeeper, he distinguished himself by his orderly habits. He carefully examined each item on every bill before approving to pay it. He was able to save $800 during his employment as an assistant bookkeeper because of his frugal lifestyle. He spent very little money on clothing; however, his clothes were always neat and clean. He had no amusements, not even the theater, but he attended every service at his Baptist Church.

He despised waste and vigilantly waged a war against all forms of wastefulness throughout his company. The following note to his barrel factory demonstrates his meticulous bookkeeping skills and shows how attentive he was to even the smallest detail involving waste:

> Last month, you reported on hand, 1,119 bungs. 10,000 were sent to you beginning this month. You have used 9,927 this month; you report 1,092 on hand. What has become of the other 100?

The missing 100-barrel bungs, worth a dollar or two at the most back then, were no laughing matter for Rockefeller. His hatred of waste told him that in large-scale industry, the rescued pennies multiplied a million times or more and represented enormous potential gains.

In his autobiography, *Random Reminiscences of Men and Events*, Rockefeller responds to accusations about Standard Oil's alleged anti-competition tactics:

> It is a common thing to hear people say that this company has crushed out its competitors. Only the uninformed could make such an assertion. It has and always has had, and always will have, hundreds of active competitors; it has lived only because it has managed its affairs well and economically and with great vigor. To speak of competition for a minute: Consider not only the able people who compete in refining oil but all the competition in the various trades which make and sell by-products—a great variety of different businesses. And perhaps of even more importance is the competition in foreign lands. The Standard is always fighting to sell the American product against the oil produced from the great fields of Russia, which struggles for the trade of Europe, and the Burma oil, which largely affects the market in India. In all these various countries we are met with tariffs, which are raised against us, local prejudices, and strange customs. In many countries we had to teach the people—the Chinese, for example—to burn oil by making lamps for them; we packed the oil to be carried by camels or on the backs of runners in the most remote portions of the world; we adapted the trade to the needs of strange folk. Every time we succeeded in a foreign land, it meant dollars brought to this country, and every time we failed, it was a loss to our nation and its workmen....The Standard has not now, and never did have a royal road to supremacy, nor is its success due to any one man, but to the multitude of able men who are working together. If the present managers of the company were to relax efforts, allow the quality of their product to degenerate, or treat their customers badly, how long would their business last? About as long as any other neglected business. To read

> some of the accounts of the affairs of the company, one would think that it had such a hold on the oil trade that the directors did little but come together and declare dividends. It is a pleasure for me to take this opportunity to pay tribute to the work these men are doing, not only for the company they serve but for the foreign trade of our country; for more than half of all the products that the company makes is sold outside of the United States. If in place of these directors, the business were taken over and run by anyone but experts, I would sell my interest for any price I could get. To succeed in a business requires the best and most earnest men to manage it, and the best men rise to the top.

I believe the foregoing passage conveys Rockefeller's thoughts on how a corporation should be managed to succeed. It clearly illustrates the importance of having a viable business model—a business can't survive without a plan to sustain it as an ongoing concern. Growth and economy of scale are essential components to providing quality products for less. This is why Rockefeller and his partners succeeded while many of his competitors failed.

Rockefeller put more emphasis on the importance of collaborative relationships than Hetty or Cornelius. Hetty had no partners and didn't collaborate with anyone. Except for Daniel Drew—who could not be trusted—Cornelius didn't have collaborative business partners either. Like Hetty and Cornelius, Rockefeller frowned upon extravagance. He had several homes, but not the extravagant variety enjoyed by so many rich people of the gilded age. In a letter to H. M. Sinclair, dated November 5, 1877, Rockefeller made the following statement:

> I have seen a good many fireplaces here [and I] don't think the character of our rooms will warrant going into the expenditures for fancy tiling and all that sort of thing that we

> find in some of the extravagant houses here. What we want is a sensible, plain arrangement in keeping with our rooms.

I think the foregoing statement is a prime example of his attitude toward the wastefulness of extravagance.

Rockefeller was a deliberate philanthropist. Hetty quietly gave money, especially to charities organized by her friend, Countess Annie Leary. Cornelius gave money on a few occasions at the prompting of his wife, Frank. Rockefeller practiced the art of giving all of his life. He retired for the sole purpose of focusing more time and effort on his acts of philanthropy.

Religion was very important to Rockefeller and may have been a great source of daily strength for him, especially when the antitrust litigation was at its zenith. Hetty had been raised as a Quaker, and I think the tenets of that faith had been embedded in her mind, although she did not formally practice Quakerism or any other religion. Cornelius stayed as far away from formal religion as possible. He was somewhat of a superstitious and mystical man. I think he relied on his faith in the supernatural and spirits to help guide him.

Wealth consciousness is a set of beliefs, habits, and behaviors that separate the wealthy from the middle class, and the poor. Hetty, Cornelius, and Rockefeller became incredibly rich because they all had a wealthy mindset. They acquired great wealth, and so can you. All you have to do is achieve wealth consciousness and take the steps you are compelled to take along the way with patience and persistence.

EPILOGUE

Acquiring Wealth Consciousness

The real difference between the wealthy and the poor is not their lifestyle but their wealth consciousness. Cornelius, Hetty, and John exhibited the wealth consciousness of the rich. For them, wealth consciousness came naturally because they had an intense desire combined with a drive to be rich. While many people may desire wealth, they lack the drive necessary to obtain it. This lack of drive can be attributable to either laziness or poverty consciousness. For those who desire to be rich but are stuck in poverty consciousness, there is good news. You can change your financial future by changing your thoughts.

Thoughts are a vital force. Although they are unseen, they are actual things, as real as the wind. They can come from within or without, and their value to any mind depends on the conditioning of that mind. You make your own poverty or wealth by the thoughts you think, which are the result of your past thoughts as well as the thoughts passed down to you from your ancestors. Your current thoughts will mold your future condition, so choose them wisely.

Building wealth is like building a house. Before you can build a house, you must draw up a blueprint that contains every room in it. Every created object takes form in the same way. The creative principle of the universe is the mind, and thought is the building material it uses. Behaviors are the tools that result from thoughts, which work to build the house.

If you have ever dreamed of being financially independent, you'll have to first develop wealth consciousness. I said, *develop,* because prosperity consciousness does not happen by chance. You are not born with it, and it cannot be given to you because it is a state of mind. To change your state of mind from one of poverty to one of wealth, you must first change your beliefs to line up with the mindset of the rich. The following five beliefs are essential in developing wealth consciousness:

> #1: A belief that there is an abundance of all good things for everyone.
>
> #2: A belief that life is fun and rewarding and that you don't have to work hard for everything you get. Money works for you, not the other way around.
>
> #3: A belief that there are many opportunities available for creating wealth.
>
> #4: A belief that you have the right to be rich and are responsible for making it so.
>
> #5: A belief that your success never prevents the success of others but may actually help others by providing jobs as well as highly demanded goods and services.

You are responsible for creating your life. Don't listen to people who tell you that you won't succeed. People who fail to acquire wealth are often easily influenced by other people's poverty consciousness. No one can hold you back. You have the power to be rich, but you must choose to be.

I wish you much success in the development of wealth consciousness and your endeavors to become financially free by choosing to be rich!

Shirley Smolko, MBA, MSA—The Venetian Medium

ABOUT THE AUTHOR

Shirley Smolko is a natural Psychic Medium, which means she was born with the ability to perceive psychic information and communicate with the souls of people who have passed away. In addition to being a Psychic Medium, she is an author, publisher, and lecturer. She holds a Bachelor of Science in Nursing, a Master's in Business Administration, and another Master's in the Science of Accounting. She enjoys writing books based on spirituality, business, and wealth creation. She lives in Venice, Florida with her husband, Joe, and two cats—Zoey and Cecilia.

List of Current Books:

- *My Adventures as a Psychic Nurse & Medium: Spirits Everywhere!* (Previously published as *Adventures of a Psychic Nurse: Spirits Everywhere!*)

- *My Adventures as a Psychic Nurse & Medium: Haunted Hospital!* (Previously published as *More Adventures of a Psychic Nurse: Haunted Hospitals!*)

- *Just a Thought Away: Communicating With Loved Ones In Spirit*

- *Money Wants Me!*

- *Money at Your Command!*

- *Secret to the Science of Getting Rich*

- *At Your Command!*

- *Revelations of the Afterlife: A New Arrival*

- *Wisdom From the Wealthy Dead: A Medium Interviews the Souls of Three American Tycoons*

You can find out more about Shirley, her itinerary, and upcoming books by going to: venetianmedium.com, or cavallaropub.com

www.ingramcontent.com/pod-product-compliance
Lightning Source LLC
Chambersburg PA
CBHW071245070526
44583CB00017B/2327